In the Blink of an Eye

Illustrated Edition

Growing Up in Rural Oxfordshire

Bill Hounslow

With additional material by Patricia Broome
Illustrated by Catherine Webber-Hounslow

In The Blink Of An Eye

In the Blink of an Eye

Cover photo:
Fawler children in Fred Able's donkey cart. The Cross, Fawler, about 1956.
Probably taken by Deena Hounslow.

In the Blink of an Eye

What is this life if, full of care,
We have no time to stand and stare.
No time to stand beneath the boughs
And stare as long as sheep or cows.
No time to see, when woods we pass,
Where squirrels hide their nuts in grass.
No time to see, in broad daylight,
Streams full of stars, like skies at night.
No time to turn at Beauty's glance,
And watch her feet, how they can dance.
No time to wait till her mouth can
Enrich that smile her eyes began.
A poor life this if, full of care,
We have no time to stand and stare.

William Henry Davies

Dedication

This book is dedicated to the memory of the people of Fawler in the 1950s and early 1960s. They were our family too.

Acknowledgements

I wish to express my thanks to my wife Catherine who has for many years been urging and encouraging me to write an account of my childhood.

I would also like to thank my sister's in law, Pauline and Therese for again allowing me to use their cottage in which to write when I needed solitude.

I am especially grateful to my sister, Patricia Broome for her invaluable recollections, some of which are included in this book.

Lastly, I am eternally grateful to my mother and father, Deena (nee Hathaway) and Frederick Hounslow, who gave me a life to write about, a childhood worth recording and the encouragement to love and understand the natural world.

Contents

Introduction

Life today in rural Oxfordshire, like much of the rest of rural Britain, bears scant resemblance to that of rural Oxfordshire in the immediate post–war years before the advent of television and the motor car.

It would be easy to present those days as some sort of idyllic golden age and for many of us life was good, relaxed and free; free from the fear of strangers that keeps so many children, rural and urban, confined to their homes or only allowed out under adult supervision. It was certainly a naive age when, even if dangers of that sort had been present, they were not talked about, being as taboo as sex, domestic violence and insanity.

It was also a time when risk was accepted and expected. Children could roam the woods and fields, climb trees, walk in fields of bullocks, swim in the river, ride home–made bikes and carts on the road and toboggan down the hills in winter, not free from risks but despite them. No parent would have thought to sue some landowner for not securely fencing off the river, putting up a sign warning of deep water or making a tree safe because a child fell in or got hurt. We expected to get hurt sometimes and learned to minimise the dangers.

I originally intended to write an account of a generalised childhood, based on the recollections of those who had lived through those times and whom I had managed to contact via the social media, but it became apparent that several were reluctant to talk about their childhood because they were not the happy, carefree days that I had remembered and had assumed theirs to have been. They did not share the same romantic memories that I and my sisters have of what, with the value of hindsight, might well have been a far from typical childhood in a far from typical close family.

Never the less, I believe it is worth placing on record what life was like for us in the small hamlet of Fawler because it is also a record of profound change. Apart from the mechanisation of agriculture, the advent of radio and the disappearance of the horse other than for recreational use, life in rural Oxfordshire in 1950 was little different to the life in rural Oxfordshire in 1850.

This account contains extracts from an unpublished memoir written by my sister, Patricia Broome. These are delineated from the main text and are given an italic font. It is sometimes difficult to know exactly where to draw the line between a full and frank account of real life and that which adds nothing but upsets and offends still–living people or their relatives. I hope I have drawn that line sensitively whilst not glossing over some of the realities of life in Fawler.

We are none of us responsible for the sins of our parents and grandparents who were shaped by forces largely outside their control. They were products of their own upbringing, the cultural assumptions of the time and the social forces of a bygone age. All families have skeletons in their cupboards. Some of them should probably stay there; many of them should not have been there anyway. Some things which were dark secrets, or which blighted the lives of innocent people, are now taken for granted in our much freer and much more liberal society.

1. Let Me Take You Home

I remember, I remember,
The house where I was born,
The little window where the sun
Came peeping in at morn...

Thomas Hood.

The River Evenlode was our playground in the long hot summer of 1959.

We spent the summer swimming, diving or lying half asleep with noses buried in fresh clover on the river bank and generally showing off to the local girls whose bodies were taking on strangely fascinating shapes. Some of the girls even began to wrap themselves in towels when they got changed. It was all very strange!

For a twelve year-old coming on thirteen these were interesting times. It was a time of change. Not just individual change but change in village life too as we ran full-tilt into the television age and the last few houses in the village got their first television sets. Life was changing forever.

We were the post–war 'Boomer' generation growing up in the small hamlet of Fawler in North Oxfordshire; an ancient little cluster of houses and a farm that can trace its origins back to at least Roman times. A hamlet that seemed wrapped up in seclusion, surrounded by woods and giant elm trees and barely noticed by passers–by on their way between Stonesfield and Charlbury or Finstock. You can pass through Fawler in the blink of an eye.

But before I get too detailed about the River Evenlode and the life along and between its banks, maybe I should introduce the hamlet of Fawler, surely one of the smaller and least important of the hamlets of North Oxfordshire.

To begin at the beginning would be difficult. No–one really knows when the beginning was because Fawler is at least Roman in origin and very probably much earlier. The name is a derivation of the Norman-French 'Fagalora' – 'coloured or spotted floor' – almost certainly a reference to the Roman mosaic floor which is said to have been excavated and removed in Victorian times.

The name is almost unique in Britain, there being only one other Fawler – a cluster of farm buildings – near Kingston Lisle in south Oxfordshire.

My Fawler – the Fawler I was born and grew up in and which was the centre of my universe for my early years – is in North Oxfordshire, southeast of the ancient Wychwood Forest. It snuggles on the road from Stonesfield to Charlbury which is imaginatively called Main Road as it passes through the hamlet. Almost all of Fawler, save a few outlying and remote farms, fits almost exactly between where the lane from Northleigh joins Main Road and where the road to Finstock forks off the Charlbury road – a distance of not more than half a mile.

Before we lost all the giant elms, Fawler seemed wrapped in a cosy blanket of woods. You might be forgiven for thinking it was the only place in the world and for us children it was certainly the most important place. It was home. It was where you came back to after school. It was the one place in the world where everyone knew you and you knew everyone.

For many years Fawler never rated a name sign to tell lost travellers where they were. When concerns for road safety became more pressing from about 1970, strangers could be forgiven for thinking they were passing through the village of 'Concealed Entrances'.

As it passes through the main part of Fawler, a lane goes left off Main Road down to The Green. This junction was and still is known as The

Cross. Not because there was a cross there but because, in earlier times, it had been a cross roads.

The Green itself was once a farm and the village green proper had been the farmyard, much of it formed more by default than design; a consequence of ill–defined property boundaries and a lack of fences. Some of it consisted of rough grass and patched of nettles which grew in abundance on ancient ash heaps. It may have been unsightly by modern standards but it was a haven for wildlife.

ooOoo

At the side of the green was a large patch of stinging nettles and behind them was an area we referred to as 'The Long Grass'. In here you could hear grasshoppers singing and of course we had to try and catch them. Finding them was easy – there were so many – but catching them was more difficult. Just as you went to grab them off they jumped into another clump of grass. Sometimes we were lucky but as we opened our hands to show someone, off they jumped again.

The other thing that lived in the Long Grass was slow worms – legless lizards that looked like small snakes. They loved to live under any large stone or in amongst the dry–stone wall that separated The Green from Mrs Rollinson's garden. Yes, you've guessed it, we had to catch them. But with care, as these clever little creature had a unique escape plan.

If you caught them by the tail, it dropped off, leaving you with just the tail wriggling in your hand and one tailless slow worm escaping into the long grass. But we knew that they were able to grow another one. If we were lucky and caught one, we put it in a shoe box with some grass, and holes made in the lid so it could breathe, and took ii home to keep as a pet, only for Mum to make us take it back down to The Green to let it go, or it mysteriously escaped over–night.

ooOoo

The 'L'–shaped former farmhouse is now three houses. A terrace of three former farm–workers cottages opposite comprises the other houses around The Green.

I've seen the lane leading to The Green called Railway Lane for no obvious reason other than that there is a railway line – the Oxford to Worcester line, part of Brunell's Great Western Railway – about 150 yards across the field from the end of the lane. We never knew it as Railway Lane and a house name was all that was needed for the postman to find our house. To us, it was, and always will be, just The Lane and our address was simply, 'Fawler, Charlbury, Oxon'. You were no good as a postman if you didn't know the names of the families in these little villages and hamlets.

The Lane was an unmade road, privately owned by the householders who lived in it and by the residents of The Green. It was not adopted by the local council until a sewerage pipe was put down the middle of it in about 1970. Until then it had been a rough stone track down which a temporary stream ran when it rained hard. After a heavy thunderstorm it would become a raging torrent for a few minutes, flooding the gardens at the end where it petered out into a garden path to the terrace. We took its roughness for granted and could run up and down it freely as children, when visiting adults trod gingerly, trying to avoid a sprained ankle.

Standing in the lane, looking across the railway and beyond I could imagine a world with castles where giants lived in clouds which scudded over Wilcote Wood beyond the railway. I can still see myself as a small child standing outside our front gate and looking at white clouds in a blue sky and wondering what was above them. In mid–afternoon, in the right conditions, sunbeams would shoot through the clouds. These were paths along which angels came to earth and the souls of dead children went to Heaven.

The village shop and bakery was a short way down The Lane. It supplied most of Fawler's groceries apart from meat and milk (which was supplied by the local farm straight from the milking parlour until that was banned because it wasn't pasteurised) and all its daily bread, as well as glorious lardy cakes, hot from the oven every Friday for six pence and almost too hot to carry home.

Our house, Scarrott's house and a couple of other houses were about half–way down The Lane. The long–redundant former Rose Public House, still known as Rose Cottage, stood at the top of The Lane. Its gardens and orchard, overgrown and with assorted outhouses in various stages of dereliction, festooned with ivy and "old man's beard" or wild clematis, extended down The Lane to almost opposite our house.

Towards Charlbury from The Cross, at the bottom of a small hill, was the telephone kiosk (the phone box) and the village letter box, opposite Manor Farm, the main farm around which modern Fawler was centred. Until the phone box was installed, the only telephone was at the farm house – only to be used in an emergency.

The farm was a mixed arable and dairy farm and supplied the village with milk directly from the dairy. One other farm, located about a mile away towards Stonesfield, farmed the fields to the east and grazed beef cattle on the water–meadows alongside the Evenlode. To us, these were "Stobo's fields" and "Creece's fields". These farms were tenants of the Blenheim Estate. A few fields and the house at Fawler Mill, towards Finstock belonged to the Cornbury Estate.

We were brought up with fields of cattle. We big, brave boys had no fear of them, of course, but the girls were afraid and needed our protection! The beef cattle, being castrated bullocks as often as heifers, were treated with a little more respect as they could be 'frisky' especially when they 'had the gad fly'. The black and white Frisian dairy cows in Creeces' field were placid and docile.

Beyond Manor Farm and at the top of a short hill were a few more ancient cottages then a cluster of four post–war 'Council Houses'. And, that was about it. In that hamlet a shade under 50 people lived, give or take the occasional death or birth, and we knew everyone.

All of the houses had large gardens because farm–workers were paid partly by land on which to grow their food. Each of them had an out–door lavatory, most of them converted to 'bucket toilets' but a few, like ours when I was young, still earth closets. All of them were well–ventilated, having holes in the doors in various shapes – diamonds, hearts, circles – and a generous gap at top and bottom. But on a hot day in summer it was still better to leave the door open.

In summer, the earth closet came alive with 'rat–tailed maggots'; the lava of the bee hoverfly, 'drone fly' or 'bind bee' that used their rat–tail to breathe through, like a snorkel. It was often wise to allow the swarm of flies gathered on the contents to disperse before settling down on the wooden seat and trapping them below you, to emerge into the daylight between your legs.

Some of the old earth closet toilets were double–seaters for the romantic couple who did everything together, and some had a smaller seat for children. It was a milestone in childhood development to be able to sit on the toilet without holding. The fear of falling in was not so much about how far you might fall but what you would fall into.

Eventually, unable to bear the shame any longer, Dad persuaded Mum to allow him to fill in the 'vault', seal it with paving slabs and install a bucket toilet, on strict condition that he emptied it every week. At least with an earth closet, the liquid soaked away; with a bucket, it just ran over! So, when I was about seven or eight, we moved up a social bracket and got a 'bucket lav'.

When I was about fourteen, we went one further and built a WC just outside the backdoor when Dad and our neighbour's son dug a septic tank and put pipes under the backyards. It was primitive but it was clean and didn't stink. What would be unacceptable today was a luxury in 1960.

Before the advent of the indoor toilet, to avoid the inconvenience of a visit to a toilet at the end of the garden in nightwear, chamber pots were normal. These were often decorated frequently with a perverse eye painted on the bottom with the words, "Thou Lord seest me". Huh? Really?

Some people find the idea of an *en suite* a little too intimate; imagine then the intimacy of a chamber pot kept under the bed and used routinely night and morning. It was usually called a 'po' or a 'guzunder' (because it guzunder the bed!). "Well, obviously!" we thought when we heard that Venice in Italy is on the River Po and often pongs in summer. Such simple pleasures!

None of the outdoor lavatories had hand basins and ideas of hygiene were primitive, so vomiting and diarrhoea, with 'eggy burps', were common. What did we know about Salmonella or E. coli? Big boils were almost a status symbol, the biggest and best being designated 'carbuncles' and proudly shown to friends. "Mine went purple and had green pus!" For some reason they seemed to grow best on the back of the neck and the upper arms.

The standard treatment was to wait until it had a good 'head' then put a 'hot poultice', i.e. a very hot flannel, on it several times. If that didn't work, then a jam jar, heated with very hot water, inverted over the boil and pressed down to seal it, often did the trick. As the air inside cooled and shrank, the partial vacuum sucked the boil out. If that didn't work, you stopped 'messing about' with it and left it till tomorrow. A particularly stubborn one might need to be lanced by the doctor. Many people sported the cross–shaped scar of a lanced boil on the back of their neck.

Sties grew on eyelids almost overnight and had to be given the wooden–spoon treatment – a handkerchief wrapped around a wooden spoon and dipped in boiling water then held as close to the sty as you could bear, until the little abscess burst. Chilblains sent my sisters mad with their itching but, for some reason I never got them. I had 'spreezed' and chapped knees in winter though and had to rub them with lanoline. We all went through measles and mumps as a matter of course, not a matter of if, but when we caught them.

Fleas, both the small black cat fleas and the larger brown human fleas, were frequently 'picked up', especially if we had been in someone else's house – as we often were. These were easily treated by sprinkling DDT powder, bought from the chemist in Charlbury, liberally in the bed. It tasted a bit strange and chalky but it only killed fleas so it must have been harmless. It was also used to treat fleas and mites on the chickens. I often wonder how much of it is still stored in my body fat.

Central heating and wall–to–wall carpets were both unknown, as was double glazing. Most houses had 'lino' on the floor at least downstairs on the concrete or even flag–stone floor. A bedside rug on the floorboards upstairs was something nice to step out of bed onto on a cold winter morning.

Draught excluders were curtains hung with brass rings on curtain rods over doorways, the only heating being a coal/wood open hearth and the only heating in a bedroom came from the hot–water bottle you took to bed with you. A few houses still had a wood–fired kitchen range. 'Jack Frost' ferns on the inside of the window on a winter morning were normal, as was ice on the wall above my bed in the bitter winter of 1963.

Most houses had a pigsty and many had a wash–house, often adjoining the toilet, and, in the case of a terrace, shared, with each house having its own wash–bowl and fire. This was where the laundry was done. We never had a pigsty or a wash–house, but we had a garage! I never knew why we had a garage – a decent–sized red–brick, tin–roofed building with room for a car and a workshop. We never had a car until about 1960 and nor had my grandparents who first lived there. I must have spent hundreds of hours in the garage on a rainy day reading old copies of Angling Times. It was where we stored sacks of potatoes, chicken corn and chicken meal, and the cats had their kittens. It was where I learned to drive a nail into wood with a hammer, use a screw driver and saw a piece of wood in half.

Pigsties, when not actually housing two or three pigs, made ideal hang–outs on wet days. The galvanized iron roofs made good slides!

Adjacent to each pigsty would be the 'muck heap', supplying an endless supply of striped red worms for fishing.

"I needs some worms fer fishin! Can I 'ave a dig in your muck 'eap?"

"'Course yer can! There's some good uns in there! Mind you leaves it tidy!"

The muck heap would be dug into the garden in autumn when the garden was 'rough–dug' and left for the winter frosts to break down into a fine tilth for seed planting. Use it for peas and beans. It's too 'hot' for spuds and encourages wireworm, and it'll make the carrots fang!

Everyone had a vegetable garden. Most families would probably not have survived without growing most of their own food. Any spare was offered around. It was almost unthinkable not to have a vegetable garden. A weed patch was a disgrace.

"Tell yer mum there a good boiling o' purple sproutin' if she wants some! Just 'elp yerself!"

"'Ow you off fer spuds this year? I can let you 'ave a bag if you want's some!"

"We got so many runner beans this year you can 'ave a pickin! Shame to let 'um go to waste!"

A good gardener knew what to plant when and how much to plant. There was no point in growing rows of cabbages or beetroot that will run to seed before you can use them. It was important to make the best use you could of the ground you had and to have something the year round.

With no freezers, having something fresh in the garden was a challenge especially in a bad year. Often root vegetables such as parsnips, carrots, swedes and turnips sustained us through the winter until the kale or sprouting broccoli came in. Surplus runner beans were salted in Kilner Jars and a good housewife – 'good' by the standards of the time – would always have something in the pantry for when the ground was too hard with frost to dig the root crops up.

In newly post–war Britain, waste was still a sin! Paper bags and string, rubber bands, wrapping paper, sugar bags, even butter and margarine wrapping papers were kept and re–used. Butter paper makes idea cake–tin lining (who on Earth buys grease–proof paper?) and sugar bags could be used to pick blackberries into. Paper bags were sandwich bags and a sandwich tin was as often as not an ancient Oxo tin with the lid held on with a rubber band.

This was a time when 'the common good' was paramount; where good neighbourliness counted for much and could be relied upon. This was the generation that had won the war and who were determined to build a better future for their children and grandchildren. They won the war and now resolved to win the peace. They elected a government pledged to raise taxes to pay for a universal health service free at the point of need and available to all. A people who believed the principles of good health, good housing, good education and freedom from want and squalor were noble aspirations and worth fighting for. Hadn't we won the war to change the world?

Many of the older people still spoke in a vernacular dialect not heard now. Words like 'bisn't', 'baint', and 'thee' were the common currency of conversation. We had a strange word for radios which we didn't even call wirelesses (they were never radios until the mid–1950s under American influence). We called it the 'wirliss'!

We also had 'shaders' for shadows, yellow was 'yaller' and lettuce with tomato and cucumber was 'sallerd'. We lived in 'air ous' with 'air Mum' and 'air Dad' and grew vegetables and reared chickens in 'air garden' or 'up air lopment' as we called our allotment on the edge of the village on the Charlbury road.

Almost all of Fawler, apart from a few privately–owned houses, was the property of the Blenheim Estate. The farms were tenant farms and the tied farm–workers cottages all belongs to the Estate, as did the village green with all its houses and the former Rose public house. Even the allotments were rented from the Estate. Consequently, property boundaries were often blurred, especially around The Green.

ooOoo

As children growing up in the fifties we had nothing: no playgrounds with slides and swings no swimming pools, no toys to ride on or fancy bikes.

In the early days we had no television. We listened to the radio. Listen with Mother at lunch lime. Children's Hour between five and six, and Uncle Mac on Saturday mornings.

We made our own entertainment out of anything we could find. We swam in the river; we ran free in the fields and woods and only came home when we were hungry. If we needed the toilet we went behind a tree and used dock leaves to clean ourselves. We played doctors and nurses, exploring our bodies and finding out the differences between boys and girls, and trying to see how they fitted together.

We felt safe and secure; nothing and nobody threatened us. We looked out for each other.

ooOoo

Apart from the shop, Fawler was served by a fish 'n chip van which came twice a week, on Tuesday evening at about 6 o'clock and Saturday morning at about 11 o'clock. A fish and chip meal was a rare treat even though a piece of battered cod cost about nine pence and chips, either three pence or six pence a bag. So a cod and chips could be bought for a shilling. If we were very lucky we might be given threepence for a thru'penny bag of chips. If we were very, very lucky, the chip man would put a few 'frazzles' in the bag. Frazzles were those bits of batter that came off the cod as it was being deep fried and had to be scooped out of the cooking oil. They even might contain a morsel of fish!

Ordering fish and chips was a ritual I could never fathom. It seems like some sort of code that I couldn't crack. People would say things like, "A fish and six twice and fish and three, three times, please!" What on Earth did this mean?

The poor old lady who lived on her pension with her disabled nephew next door to us made the mistake of giving me a pound note and asking me to run up to the chip van on Saturday morning and get her a 'fish and six and a fish and three', so, unable to work out what I was supposed to buy, I bought six pieces of fish and three bags of chips.

I can still hear her now!

"Look what this bloody silly bugger's bin and bought me! He's spent all me pension! What do I need all that fish for you stupid little bugger?! Deena! Come out here and look at what this bloody idiot's done!" Deena was my mother.

She even tried haranguing and begging the hapless milkman, Harold, who happened to be delivering at the time, to buy a piece of fish. To her credit, she never used the 'f' word. Or maybe she did and I didn't know what it meant.

In the end, our mother bought four pieces of fish and a bag of chips from her and I had to do extra chores to pay her back, and go without pocket money for a week. The fish was a treat though! It was probably the major event in the hamlet that week.

The other regular visiting trader was 'The Friday Man', who did a round every Friday evening at about five o'clock, and parked up on The Green after ringing his bell. He sold hardware and just about anything you needed. If he didn't have it, he would get it for next week. A pound of oval nails; a roll of chicken wire; a zinc bath; a hand axe; a pair of brass hinges; enamelled plates and mugs; cans of 3 in 1 cycle oil; bicycle chains; fire–lighters, even a length of catapult elastic.

"I need twenty yards of six foot, two inch chicken wire. You got any?"

"I can get it fer next week! That okay? Dju need any staples?"

He sold paraffin too; pink paraffin that he dispensed from a large drum through a funnel with a filter in it which made it foam up, but the foam went quickly, unlike soapy foam. These things are important to an inquisitive mind!

The Friday Man's red van was a sight to behold, festooned with rolls of chicken wire, buckets, large and small zinc baths, sheets of galvanised iron; some on the roof, some hanging from the back doors and some, like ladders or bundles of bean canes, tied to the side.

In time immemorial – which for us was mostly a time before Gran Scarrott could remember – there had been some sort of industry at Fawler. In the woods between the hamlet proper and Fawler Mill were the remains of a brick kiln and the roofless remains of buildings. This had even rated a spur–line off the railway which had run between man–made embankments. At the place where the spur had branched off the main line stood a stone–built, slate–rooved hut complete with fire–place and chimney, presumably where the man who operated the points spent his working day.

In the wood around the brick kiln were the scars of quarrying now overgrown with trees hanging with thick ropes of wild clematis which we called Tarzan creeper. It was usually strong enough for us to swing on. The top of the old quarry face was protected only by a wire fence, the post of which were loose and rotted, and often hanging in the air, the soil in which they had once been embedded having fallen into the quarry. As children, we knew we shouldn't cross this fence, as the soil could easily 'cave in' hurling us to a certain death into the woods below. At the edge of the field we were almost level with the tree tops.

There were the remains of another quarry behind the farm through a pine wood we called The Spinney. It was here that I found some of my best fossils and where, as a teenager, I took the grandsons of the then famous scientists and greatest paleoanthropologist of his day, Professor Sir Wilfred Le Gros Clarke, to look for fossils.

Sir Wilfred, Professor of Anatomy at Oxford and one of the team who proved Piltdown Man to be a hoax, had moved into a newly–built house in Fawler some years earlier. I first met him when he and his wife stayed in the cottage belonging to another scientist while she was away for a year. I delivered their Sunday newspapers. This scientist was Dr Alice Stewart who first used the computing power of the multi–million pound Oxford University computer to prove the link between smoking and lung cancer. She is remembered in Fawler by a memorial bench on The Green.

The Le Gros Clarke's house was the only new house to be built in Fawler since the council houses had been built just before I was born. Its building was accompanied by considerable regret and hostility from us children because the garden had incorporated the Big Tree, an isolated elm, the climbing of which was a milestone in childhood. It had been our playground for years and now stood behind a fence. It succumbed to Dutch elm disease in about 1974.

Sir Wilfred and his wife became good friends who encouraged my love of nature and gave me free use of their massive library. They had so many books they actually had a private library in their house! He gave me a book–case in which I proudly displayed my collection of Observer's books and books about birds, fishes and nature in general. I still have this lovely little arts and crafts bookcase. He also gave me what seemed like hundreds of postage stamps from all over the world, especially at Christmas. I was an inveterate collector of many things.

He had no doubt at all that humans were apes that had evolved slowly over millions of years in Africa. He had written the British Museum's definitive guide to the evolution of man and I still have my signed copy.

So that, in a nutshell, and it would just about fit into a nutshell, maybe a large one, was Fawler in the late 1950s, the centre of my universe. It was a not quite self–sufficient community, where feral children roamed the woods and fields free from fear of strangers and mostly free from the encumbrance of possessions and designer labels.

It was a way of life probably having more in common with the world of 1817 than the world of 2017.

In The Blink Of An Eye

2. Evenlode Days

The tender Evenlode that makes
Her meadows hush to hear the sound
Of waters mingling in the brakes,
And binds my heart to English ground.

A lovely river, all alone,
She lingers in the hills and holds
A hundred little towns of stone,
Forgotten in the western wolds.

Hilaire Belloc

For nearly twenty years, the River Evenlode had been firmly in the centre of my world. Not only had it been our playground in the summer, once we had had enough days of sunshine to raise the temperature enough to make it tolerable, but it also provided somewhere to sit, fishing-rod in hand or propped up on a rod-rest, and quietly watch nature go by.

The Evenlode is one of four main rivers that, together with the Thames of which they are tributary, drain out of the Cotswold to the Northwest and flow roughly southeast, joining up to flow through Oxford as the Isis, through the Chiltern Hills at Goring and on to London as the Thame.

These rivers have flowed since at least the last Ice Age and have formed the ancient water meadows and alluvial soils on which the prosperity of the area depended. With the ancient woodlands, this part of England is amongst the most bio–diverse in Europe, home to a rich variety of vertebrate, invertebrate and plant life, both aquatic and terrestrial.

We would stay in the river on a hot day until the herd of dairy cows, thirsty and fresh out of the milking parlour, looking for somewhere cool in the heat of the afternoon, waded into the shallows and under the shade of the railway bridge. We would hang on just a little longer until the water turned a nasty shade of greenish–yellow and became too turbid to swim and dive in.

With no showers in any of the houses, and very few with hot water, this was going to need a strip-wash with a soapy flannel or a cold bath when we got home. It was not going to wait till Saturday bath night!

ooOoo

At the bottom of the lane and across Creese's field was the River Evenlode. From the youngest age we were taken down to paddle. The shallowest part was called Dunford. If you stayed near the bank you were fine. The older ones who could swim went across to the other side were it was deeper.

I can remember my brother falling in and going under the water. Mum had to jump in to save him. It was a good job she could touch the bottom, as she never learnt to swim.

In the summer all the mums and dads came and sat on the river bank and chattered and kept a close eye on us. Aunty Mill or Aunty Brenda made a tray of tea and it turned in to quite a social gathering.

As we got older we progressed up river to the "Swerly'. This was a very deep area just below the arch. We had to learn to swim before we were allowed in this part. The oldest taught the youngest. Mary and Lilian taught me. As you climbed into the river from the bank it was shallow but suddenly you went down a ledge and it was so deep you couldn't touch the bottom. On the opposite side, against the bank, grew a clump of reeds. We used to pull these and tie them together and make

*a float. You could also dive in from this bank. Bill and the older ones
made a wooden jetty that stuck out into the river. This made an even
better diving board.*

*We used to go up the dump at the top barns and find old oil drums –
four if possible – rope them together and tie planks of wood on the top
to make a raft and then climb on it only to dive off again time and time
again, or see how far down the river we could get before it fell to pieces
or we fell off.*

*Once, Mr Goodwin gave us a tractor tyre inner tube. They were huge.
We patched it up and when blown up, there was room for several of us
to spend hours laying on it, drifting about aimlessly.*

*If the river weed grew too thick we pulled it out by the arm full so
keeping a large area free for us to play in.*

ooOoo

From the railway bridge, the Evenlode continued its slow, lazy summer
meander through water–meadows and woods where dairy cows and
beef cattle grazed in summer. Before reaching Fawler, from its origins
in the Gloucestershire Cotswolds at the village of Evenlode, it had
looped and twisted in a slow meander across North Oxfordshire through
chains of similar water-meadows and the grounds of country houses.

A regular intervals these natural meanders had been exploited in a
bygone age to create the mill-streams and water mills which had once
been a feature of the pre-industrial English rural scene, powering the
mills that ground the wheat to make the daily bread. They were
harnessing the free, renewable energy that fell as rain, usually
plentifully, and adding to the diversity of water habitats with mill–races,
mill–pools and back–waters.

The main river had been dammed to raise its level and diverted to
power a water wheel. The original course now merely took the

overflow which topped the dam when the river level was high enough or seeped around the edge, resulting in a quiet backwater, often consisting of isolated pools supplied only with a trickle. In places the original dam had simply fallen into disuse and degenerated.

Wildlife teemed in these backwaters, including, in at least one section, a population of lampreys that could sometimes be flushed out from underneath larger stones. The streams were often lined with yellow-flag irises, bull–rushes and burr reeds and were havens for moorhens, mallards and dabchicks as we called little grebes. Watercress could be gathered in great bunches in the shallows and within a few days would be ready to be picked again.

Like a great deal of the Evenlode, these mill-streams were often lined with pollard willow from a time when good, straight willow poles were an important crop. By the 1950s many of these were no longer cropped and had split or rotted away at the heart to form hollow trees.

The gnarled heads of these old willows provided a great profusion of nesting sites for birds and almost anything that could take root in the head would be found growing there, from wild roses, blackberries, red and black currents and gooseberries to elder. Scarcely a single willow would be without a bird's nest or two, if you searched carefully and knew where to look.

Apart from human engineering and the course of little feeder streams, the water meadows were as flat as billiard tables, being made over tens of thousands of years by alluvial silt deposits in the winter floods.

The Evenlode was a bright, clear, sparkling river where pike and chub could be seen in the shallows between mats of white–flowered water crowfoot, and crayfish could be caught in abundance in the stony shallows, where a pair of rubber wellies was usually enough to wade across. The crayfish were simply picked up and popped into a bucket! Boiled up over a wood fire they would make a delicious casual snack.

Then one day the crayfish were all gone!

We caught bullheads and loaches in glass jam-jars, not for food but for the fun of it. The trick was to turn the stone over downstream so any disturbed mud and sand immediately washed away. The jar was then carefully placed behind the fish – which always face upstream – and the cupped hand slowly advanced towards it. Loach and bullheads rely on cryptic camouflage so only swim away as you almost touch them – straight into the jam-jar.

Judging by the crayfish claws and macerated bullheads I found in the stomachs of eels, they were the staple diet that would build the eel's body over several years until it had enough fat to sustain it for its long journey to the Sargasso Sea.

During this journey, the eels would stop eating, absorb their own digestive systems and convert their bodies to living in salt water. They would never return to the rivers they had grown up in since the elvers made their way there from the Sargasso Sea. A very good Evenlode eel was about two pounds in weight, sometimes two and a half or even three. The smaller ones made the best jellied eel though because they were not too fatty.

Just sitting and watching on a quiet river-bank in summer surely has few equals for relaxation! Who needs yoga and transcendental meditation when you have a quiet stretch of water crowfoot, preferably flanked with stiff, bright green swords of bur reed? The gentle swaying in the river current of the long feather fronds of water crowfoot is hypnotic. The gentle sough of the wind in the rushes is equal to anything people will pay good money to a pharmacist or a personal trainer, or possibly both, for!

Although this stretch of the Evenlode looked perfectly natural, in fact its present course is recent; it was diverted to make the railway bridges easier to build. The clue is that the river normally runs straight under the bridge at right-angles to the railway line and so needs the shortest bridge.

The Evenlode in our local field had been diverted right through the remains of a Roman Villa from which the hamlet indirectly takes its name as I mentioned earlier. The Roman mosaic was supposedly uncovered then covered over again in about 1865. Another Roman mosaic from the same villa was destroyed during the building of the Oxford to Worcester railway line.

A further trace of Roman activity in the Hamlet could be heard in the local name of a now closed footpath known to the locals as 'Vizziker' which ran down to the Green from near where Main Road forks to Stonesfield and North Leigh, to continue across the Green, over a now-overgrown stile and across the meadow to the river. Here it originally crossed 'Fawler Bridge' to run up to Finstock with a fork to Wilcote. In the other direction from the Main Road it ran across to the later Stonesfield slate pits towards Hill Barn Farm and to join up with the old road from Stonesfield to Charlbury.

Vizziker is very probably a contraction of the Latin 'Via Dessica' (Dry Way). Sadly, the landowner (the local shopkeeper) down the side of whose garden Vizziker ran, succeeded in closing it in the 1960s for long enough to close it permanently, and Vizziker, the two thousand year old Roman Dry Way, passed out of folk memory and off the footpath maps for ever.

'Fawler Bridge' was first recorded in 1298. It is difficult to work out exactly where this bridge was. Given the alignment of the footpath across the meadow and the footpaths to Finstock and Wilcote, it seems likely that the bridge either crossed the river where the present railway bridge is, or further upstream where the Evenlode takes a sharp left as it comes up against the wooded hill known officially as Dunford Copse (although never known by that name to us).

Either way, there was no trace of this bridge in the 1950s. The only way to cross the river was to trespass on the railway line, or to wade across the shallows near the railway bridge – only possible sometimes in a very dry summer. We kept trying to make stepping stones across these shallows but the stones were not big enough and got washed away in the winter floods. A nice new footbridge now spans the river just the other side of the railway bridge.

Soon after the Evenlode flows under the railway bridge it takes a sharp right turn, digging into the left-hand bank and producing the 'Swirly' which legend had it was bottomless. It wasn't, of course; it was about six or seven feet deep, eight at the most, but the legend was enough to deter small children from trying to swim in it. The Swirly was for big children and adults. Being able to dive to the bottom and bring up a stone to prove it was a definite status symbol given to only a few of us.

Smaller children swam further down or played on a shallow sandbank just below the Swirly. How did we learn to swim? We took a good bunch of the broad–leaved burr–rushes, tied more rushes round them to make a float, and lay across it! Pretty soon we realised we didn't need the bundle of rushes.

It was in this 'safe' part of the river, in a stretch we call Dunford that the small children paddled and played and even tried to make sandcastles from the river sand in the shallows. A thick mat of pulled–up water crowfoot or rushes made it less muddy to go in and out of the river and a handy fallen willow tree provided seats for mothers and grans.

It was here that as a three year-old I was pulled out from underwater by my mother as I was rolling along the bottom. I still remember that strange sensation of rolling along the bottom of the river, then suddenly being swept up and wrapped in towels, coughing and spluttering while mother complained of having got her dress soaked. For some reason, as I recall things, it took a lot of towels to wrap me in, provided by the other mothers and assorted grans. My older sister took the brunt of the blame because she should have made sure I was in the shallows when, playing ring-a-ring-a-roses, we all fell down. My older sister was about eight, maybe nine!

The strange thing is I don't recall being afraid when I was under water. I was probably oblivious of the danger I was in.

This was not the only time I scared my mother over drowning in the river. It seemed to be an ever-present threat to our parents but a danger which to us children with our sense of immortality, just did not exist. I had gone down to the river ahead of my sisters and mother, dressed only in bathing trunks and sandals.

I slipped off my sandals and jumped in then noticed a section of the railway embankment on fire a couple of hundred yards along from the bridge. This was a regular occurrence in the days of steam when the vegetation used to be scythed down and left. The fires normally just burned themselves out eventually.

So, having spotted this small fire, and having wet feet, I never bother putting my sandals on and ran along the railway track in my trunks and bare feet, leaving my sandals on the river-bank – where my mother found them.

I was nowhere to be seen.

Obviously, I was not going to go anywhere without my sandals on!

Obviously, I was on the river-bed, having dived in and hit my head! It was the only possible explanation!

Then I came happily jogging back along the railway track to the extraordinary sight of a distraught mother and sisters! I got such a loving clout, heard my mother use some words I had never heard before, got called an idiot yet again – and we went straight home. Only the village idiot would go running off along a railway track in bare feet! What did I think I was playing at?!

I couldn't see what all the fuss was about! Anyone could have worked out that if the railway embankment was on fire, I would go to watch it! And how could I put sandals on when my feet were wet and I hadn't even taken a towel? Why on earth would I dive in and hit my head in the 'bottomless' Swirly! Women! They are so unreasonable! They just never think things through!

The Evenlode teamed with wildlife, both in the water and on the banks. There was endless fascination from just turning over a stone and looking for the different cadis fly lava. Some used small stones and grains of sand to make their protective case and others used short lengths of plant material. I didn't appreciate at the time that these were different species. I just found it fascinating how different ones used different building materials all stuck together with silk and surprisingly tough.

Occasionally, there were huge hatchings of mayflies when they hung in bunches from the trees or flew, mating on the wing, in great pale yellow clouds. The chub fed to their fill as no doubt did the few brown trout as the surface of the river was littered with egg-laying females or dead or dying spent individuals. Sparrows darted out to skilfully take them on the wing. I could almost imagine an over-fed chub coming to the surface to burp!

Mayflies take several years as aquatic nymph before reaching maturity, to hatch over a few days in May, mate, lay eggs and die in about a day. A great cycle of life that has been going on in streams since the *Ephemera* first appeared in the Carboniferous Era when the vertebrates were only just beginning to transition from fish into salamander-like terrestrial animals, long before there were dinosaurs let alone mammals or English water–meadows.

And then in a couple of days the mayfly hatching was over, the next generation committed to the tender mercies of just about any predator such as dragonfly and water-beetle lava, and the few dippers that occasionally appeared on the Evenlode. Natural selection had applied the selective sieve of fitness to the next generation and only the survivors would survive to do it all again. In a classic selfish gene strategy all that matters is that enough new individuals are produced each generation to sustain the genepool. Sacrificing maybe ninety percent or more of each generation in the process is of no concern to mayfly genes.

The mayflies too suddenly disappeared as quickly as the crayfish, so after about 1960 I never saw another one on the Evenlode and have never again witness one of these mass hatchings on this scale. Like all predator-prey relationships, populations are subject to rapid annual fluctuation with booms and busts common, so maybe the vast mayfly swarms in the late 1950s were the exception.

The Evenlode has several moods. In summer it is languid and calm, fringed with rushes and covered in the shallower places with gently wafting white-flowered water crowfoot, interspersed with little rivulets, yellow, almond–scented water lilies with their round pads in the slightly deeper parts and patches of open water in the deeps.

Water crowfoot often provides a feeding place for roach and dace, hidden from watching herons. It is in these places that a carefully placed fishing line baited with a small worm or pellet of bread paste, the float just off the downstream edge of the weed, will stand a good chance of taking a few roach, provided pesky minnows don't strip the hook first.

Dace make up a catch but were always returned as inedible and not worth the cooking. Roach, if they're not too big, can be reasonably good to eat, if a little muddy. A good Evenlode roach would have been about one and a half pounds (about three quarters of a kilo). Chub on the other hand were considerably bigger and could be seen in small shoals when the water was clear, with their characteristic black fins and tail and big, white mouth.

Chub could be taken by floating a hook baited with a piece of bread paste about the size of a thumb nail down into the shoal. A good chub could be two to three pounds (roughly one to one and a half kilo). An old country recipe for preparing chub is to de-scale, de-head and gut the chub, lay it in the middle of a wooden board, cover it with herbs and spices - whatever is to hand – season well, cover and bake in a moderate oven for four hours. Then remove from the oven, scrape the chub and herbs into a bin and eat the wood. It is bound to be better than the taste of sharp needles wrapped in muddy cotton wool.

Apart from the very occasional small brown trout and eels, the only other fish worth catching for the pot were pike and perch. I only ever caught perch in a single spot about a mile or so downstream from Fawler, on both occasions when 'bottom fishing' for eels with a worm bait.

Fishing for us Fawler children was a very unfussy affair done without ceremony or paraphernalia. My first rod was two bean-canes joined with a metal ferule and with a bamboo handle, and wire eyes taped on with electrical tape. The top ring was the key from a corned beef tin, hammered into the end of the cane and bent at right-angles. The reel was a plastic centre-pin reel with about fifty feet of nylon line, weights were assorted nuts and bolts from a Meccano set and the float was as often as not a stick or a stick pushed through a cork.

I later bought a fixed spool 'self-caster' from a left-handed friend who taught me how to cast in the middle of a field. It was only as an adult that I realised I had been fishing left-handed for most of my life.

My best friend's rod was made from a hazel pole cut from a hedge, with staples for eyes and a cheap plastic reel. Somehow, even with that, he manged to hook and land a three-pound eel and a twelve-pound pike. Later on, when we were older we would cycle over to Witney to Bob Bridgeman's fishing shop in Bridge Street and buy such previously undreamed of luxuries as Mepp's spinners in a range of sizes, packets of pre-tied hooks, colourful floats, lengths of nylon line and split lead-shot weights. Until then, these things had been currency with bird's eggs, foreign stamps, etc. being exchanged for split rings, swivels, hooks, or even for something especially prized – a Mepp's No.1 spinner.

Without a box of tackle, treeing your line or losing it by snagging a lily pad stalk, or even being broken up by a "big 'un'" meant an end to the day's fishing and being out of action until you could cadge a replacement hook. So keen was I not to lose my line that I frequently stripped off and swam down to free it by hand. Well, some things are important!

My old bean-cane rod finally met its match when a spinner was taken by an enormous pike in a small patch of clear water surrounded by weeds. In trying desperately to keep it from the weeds and bring it close enough to the bank to land it, the top section snapped just above the ferule, the pike had a clear run and snapped the line like cotton, leaving me to raise everyone's eyebrows with the tale of the one that got away. "Honestly! It had a mouth like a crocodile and was miles bigger than David Miller's eighteen–pounder". It was pretty big though!

One good way to lose a hook was to try to land an eel up a steep bank without a landing net. Eels are highly intelligent and, when they feel the hook pulling them will reach their tail round over the line and try to pull the hook out of their mouth. The only way to prevent this is to relax the line; but you have to have a tight line to land the eel. If you are unlucky either the line snaps or the hook pulls out. On occasion, even the hook itself will snap. I have lost many a hook and eel this way.

But as I grew up and my appreciation of nature and wildlife changed so my attitude toward it changed. Previously, I have been an avid collector of birds' eggs (when it was still legal), would set a ferret down a rabbit burrow and dispatch any rabbits that popped up into the nets placed over the holes, could and did set rabbit snares in hedgerows where there were rabbit runs and shot sparrows, rooks and wood pigeons with an air-rifle or a 4.10 shotgun for the sport of it.

Then something happened I have never forgotten and which still fills me with shame to this day. I was out with a mate carrying our home-made catapults when I saw a moorhen on the far side of the local pond. Without thinking I let fly with a glass marble from the catapult. It was the perfect shot, hitting the moorhen on the head and either killing it or stunning it and its head went under water. Before we could get to the other side it was dead. I picked it up and couldn't believe that I had thoughtlessly ended the life of such a beautiful creature.

I made a promise to the dead moorhen that I would never needlessly take the life of another living creature. It is not something I am fanatical or obsessive about and not something I go on about; just a private thing between me and a dead moorhen. It was the very least I could do.

Life is too rare, precious and wonderful a thing to be taken lightly. I do not believe we have dominion over other animals and that they are ours to use as we wish. They are their own and deserve to live. It was only then that my mother's saying made real sense to me – "Everything has a right to life. They're not yours, they're theirs!"

I went home and put an exe to my catapult.

After that I rarely fished and, when I did, fish were returned to the water straight away unless they promised exceptionally good eating. The riverbank for me became a place of quiet contemplation or as a teenager, somewhere to sit and canoodle with a girlfriend. I did some of my best studying for 'O' Levels on the riverbank near my favourite sycamore tree, opposite where a spring welled up from under a big ironstone bolder in a thicket of trees and merrily trickled the twenty or so yards to the river.

This thicket was where, years earlier, we had made a fire and cooked a partridge and went home smelling of wood smoke. It was where we almost succeeded in taming a robin enough to take food from our hands. With mealworms, we would probably have won it over completely. Alas, all we had to offer was white bread from the pack of cheese sandwiches mother had given us so we did not go hungry.

It was near that spot that I saw a couple of extraordinary things. I saw a magnificent male stoat run across the surface of the mat of water crowfoot, running so fast that it did not have time to sink through. Just a few moments later, it climbed up to the flat top of a fence-post and, standing on its hind legs and stretching up as far as possible, it took a slow full three hundred and sixty degree survey of its domain, and then scampered back down again and away.

On another occasion, sitting quietly and revising for a chemistry exam, I heard a massive splash as a black and white Frisian dairy cow lost its footing on the bank and fell, legs in the air, into the river. Luckily the river at that point was shallow enough for it to find its footing, clamber up the bank and continue grazing as though that was all part of a plan and it had been perfecting that trick for some time. I just wish someone else had been there to share it.

Characteristic of the Evenlode, and probably of most southern English rivers, was the plop of a diving water vole as you walked by. I will not call them 'water rats' as they were usually called because that maligns a harmless little creature that is not a rat at all but our largest vole. They are no more rats that field voles are mice. The riverbank teamed with them to the extent that people said they undermined the bank and cause it to collapse. They were almost universally known as water rats – an unfortunate association, being wholly vegetarian and no threat to human health in the least.

They are sadly almost extinct on many rivers now for reasons which I will elaborate on later. Suffice it to say at this point that it is wholly an unintended consequence of human interference.

Just occasionally, if you were very lucky and observant, you could see our largest shrew, the very beautiful black and silver water shrew. This shrew hunted equally happily on the river bed for cadis fly, fresh-water shrimps and beetle larvae or on the bank for earworms and snails. They would even take unsuspecting frogs and fishes.

Apart from their dense fur, the only concession to an aquatic lifestyle these shrews make is not by having webbed feet but by having a margin of stiff, short hairs on the margins of the feet and as a keel on their tail.

My relationship with hedgehogs had always been a cordial one. I had no reason to bear them ill will and every reason to want to encourage them to come into our gardens to eat the slugs and other garden pests, but this goodwill was put the test one summer afternoon on the banks of the Swirly. Like everyone else, I was barefoot and in swimming gear when someone spotted a hedgehog swimming along the far side of the river just beneath the bank. Having proceeded a certain distance, and with clear malice aforethought, it turned purposefully across the river, climbed up the bank, walked some ten yards along to me - and gave me a very painful bite on the little toe.

I don't know what I did or said to deserve it but everyone else thought it was hilarious. Was it something I said; the way I looked; a faint smell, maybe? Had I done something socially unacceptable in polite hedgehog circles? I never did find out, but the hedgehog, apparently satisfied with its endeavours, waddled off along the river bank as though putting an adolescent human male in his place with a painful bite was all in a day's work and certainly well worth swimming across the Evenlode for.

We had names for most of the sections of the Evenlode, as least insofar as it ran through our neck of the woods. As well as the Swirly and Dunford, we all knew precisely where First Hole, Roach Hole, Sycamore, First Bend and Second Bend were. Downstream, we knew Willows, Hawthorn and of course, Second Bridge.

But before all this chit-chat about fishing intruded I was writing about the moods of the Evenlode.

As the summer ended and the days shortened, the Evenlode began to go into its autumn and winter mood. The water crowfoot died down, the yellow water lilies and rushes were no more. The Evenlode began to prepare for its main function in life – to spread a fine layer of nutrient silt over the water meadows and so ensure another generation of grazing for dairy and beef cattle and another year of the biodiversity which had sustained these ancient water meadows since long before Man appeared on the scene in post-glacial Britain.

As the rains of late summer and autumn swelled the Evenlode, our once tranquil, rush-lined, sparkling stream of bright water turned muddy brown as the water level rose. Small lakes appeared in fields which had been dry in summer.

After a few days of heavy rain the Evenlode would 'break its banks' and flood the water-meadows, depositing its precious cargo of silt and nutrients to sustain the grass for another year. A good covering of grass binds the soil and prevents it being washed away while slowing down the flow of flood water causing it to drop its load. Later on, the population of earthworms would incorporate this new deposit into the rich loam where it sustains one of the most diverse ecosystems found in Britain.

Probably the two largest single stretches of ancient water-meadow around Fawler were the meadow under the railway bridge and the meadow through which the Evenlode flowed on its way to the second railway bridge. Both of these were put to the plough in a search of a quick profit, with no regard to what was being irrevocably destroyed in a single year. Now the winter floods, instead of enriching and renewing the soil, leeches the nutrients out and washes them away along with the top–soli. Some of it will find its way into other water-meadows of course, but much of it will add to the silting up of the lower Evenlode and the Thames, increasing the risk of flooding in the town centres.

These water-meadows are such a characteristic part of the English countryside and are so essential for maintaining biodiversity that I believe they should be listed and protected like listed buildings. The idea that someone in search of a quick cash-crop like rapeseed can simply destroy a hundred thousand years of natural creativity in a year is awful! We owe it to our children and our grandchildren and to the wildlife with which we share this planet to preserve these water-meadows.

As I argued in my anti–religious polemic, *Ten Reasons To Lose Faith*, the notion that the planet belongs to humans to do with as we wish was never more than a faith-based notion deriving from the Bible and having its origins in Mesopotamian mythology. As such, in my opinion, it is one of the most destructive of religious dogmas and needs to be abandoned.

We must accept that we and all of nature share this planet and have the great good fortune to experience it briefly. With our cavalier attitude we are not being agents of preservation and guardianship; we are active agents of destruction.

I was becoming vaguely aware of the issue of the 'ownership' of the countryside and wildlife in particular as a child growing up. Having realised I was an atheist at the age of nine I felt no obligation to subscribe to these dogmas but was free to think about things and form my own opinions. I found it hard to accept, for example, that only humans are sentient, that only humans can feel love for their children and their mates, or that only humans have any idea of death. To me, these seemed nothing more than arrogant assumptions intended to make us feel that little bit more important, as though simply being alive is not important enough.

The Evenlode epitomised this idea of common heritage to me. It has been there, flowing across North Oxfordshire since the last Ice Age, slowly creating its water-meadows and carving out its meandering bed maybe since before modern humans came into the island and probably before the North Sea finally broke through at Dover, cutting us off from the rest of Europe. The diverse wildlife on it and in the water-meadows was the descendants of the first fauna to re-populate the island after the ice retreated.

They were not ours; they were theirs!

And so back to the moods of the Evenlode from which reality keeps diverting me with all her talk of wildlife, biodiversity and politics.

As the winter floods subsided, leaving some isolated pools which, if we had a few sharp frosts in winter, would serve as skating rinks, though none of us had skates. For some reason we were always terrified of 'going through the ice' because we would surely drown, even though the water was no more than a couple of feet deep and would hardly cover your welly tops. With a stick each and a chunk of ice as a puck, we could have a decent game of ice-hockey.

In the 1950s the now-common sight of gulls in North Oxfordshire was a rarity. They were only ever seen at the seaside so were called seagulls. I saw my first black-headed gull on the semi-permanent winter flood, although it did not have the full black head, only the dark smudge behind its eye of its winter plumage. I was awestruck by the sheer beauty of a gull in flight, white against an azure–blue sky, with its thin, sickle–shaped wings and easy, souring flight. I stood entranced for what seemed like an age, hoping it would not fly away.

My mother, steeped in weather lore she got from her shepherd father, said it was a sign of bad weather coming when the gulls came inland. So it might have been once upon a time; it's now a sign of reservoirs, rubbish tips and other trappings of urbanisation.

So the waters of the Evenlode subsided as spring came with its promise of summer. The turbid water began to clear and fairly soon the rushes would begin to show, lily pads began to appear and the water crowfoot would start to form the familiar summer mats. Somehow, the fish had managed not to get washed away and were still to be seen in the shallows. Fairly soon the sparkling bright Evenlode was back to her friendly and inviting self again.

And so the bright sparkling Evenlode was central to our lives growing up in Fawler, especially before television came to dominate our lives and we turned our backs on our faithful old friend. She gave us so much and asked for nothing in return apart from being loved and respected, valued for who she was and to be allowed to continue being what she had been for a hundred thousand years and not to become just another polluted drainage ditch serving the needs of industrialised agriculture.

3. Dam Builders and Ship Wrights

"Believe me, my young friend,
there is nothing – absolutely nothing –
half so much worth doing
as simply messing about in boats."

Kenneth Grahame,
The Wind in the Willows

We were industrious engineers on the Evenlode.

We built dams across the shallows just below the Swirly to help raise the water level for swimming. The technique was simple, in principle. We put a line of large stones across the river from bank to bank, curved into the current. Then we put other stones across the gaps on the upstream side and piled more stones up as necessary. Finally, armfuls of water crowfoot were packed up again the upstream side to seal the gaps between the stones.

The problem always was in getting the last few stones into place as the weight of water increased. So successful was one particular effort one year that the water pouring through the gap between the end of the dam and the high bank on the far side undermined the bank, causing several yards of it to collapsed, exposing a seam of alluvial gravel. Much of this was deposited immediately beyond the dam, serendipitously forming a nice sandbank for the smaller children to play on.

When we are older we also made rafts out of willow poles and large metal drums of various sizes we found in the refuse tip from the local farm. We had no idea what hazardous chemicals had been in these drums but the largest raft we made was a huge 'fifteen canner' which would safely take four or five of us. We punted it along with a couple of long willow poles and only needed to get off and manhandle it in the shallows under the railway bridges, unless the water was high enough to shoot through in the deepest place.

Sometimes cans would fill with water and we would need to haul the raft out and empty them. This often left a patch of dead grass where we had emptied the contents! We really were oblivious to the risks we were taking. This was in the days before compulsory hazard warnings and with little in the way of health and safety awareness or environmental sensitivity. I just hope we didn't add too much to whatever was by now finding its way into the bright, sparkling Evenlode and beginning to turn its clear summer water a rather murky green so that it quickly became impossible to see the fish in the shallows as we strolled along its banks.

But, gently floating along the Evenlode on a raft is almost as relaxing as sitting on her banks. Fish seem to be programmed to be wary of an upright figure on the bank, probably because it means 'heron' but they seem to have no such fear of someone on a raft, probably because it is just a lump of flotsam to them. So, you can watch the fish very easily from a raft as they swim underneath and around it, completely unconcerned by your presence.

The twine we used for the raft was coarse bailer twine which we got in vast quantities from the same farm spoil tip we got the drums from. The short lengths cut from hay bales were joined together and plaited to make stronger ropes but it was never intended to be used in water. It came apart and rotted very quickly so we were lucky if a raft lasted the winter. The 'fifteen canner' disappeared one night during the floods and was never seen again. I used to fondly imagine it turning up in Tilbury Dock or maybe making it to France. In all probability it never got past Ashford Mill a couple of miles downstream.

It was in the long hot summer of 1959 that we learned a valuable lesson. As Robert Burns put it, "The best laid plans o' mice an' men gang aft agley." Burns was talking to a mouse. It is unlikely that he ever decided to make a log boat, but we decided we were going to. It would make the ideal toy in the river as we sat astride it with a fence railing or piece of board each for a paddle.

Having carefully selected an elm sapling, nice and straight, free from too many branches lower down and about eighteen inches thick at the base, we set about chopping it down. It was about two hundred yards from the river and about half a mile downstream from the Swirly, but we had a cunning plan.

With a hand axe each we hacked away for most of the morning, being careful to make sure we cut on the side we wanted it to fall towards so it wouldn't get caught up in the surrounding trees. We were nothing if not careful planners. By about mid-day we had the tree down and the branches trimmed off, with just the top section to detach to leave a nice straight trunk about ten feet long – plenty of room for three of four to sit astride.

All we had to do was carry it the two hundred yards to the river.

We couldn't lift it! Wood is supposed to be light!

Undaunted, we rolled it across the water-meadow in the heat of the afternoon, dripping with sweat and with aching limbs and backs, but we were not going to be deprived of our prize and the fruits of our labour. This was going to be a summer to remember!

The plan was to ceremonially launch the log boat by rolling it the last final push off the river bank, then ride it triumphantly up to the Swirly.

One last big push! "I name this ship *Logboat!*"

We never saw it again. It sank like a stone. A sappy elm sapling in mid-summer is heavier than water!

Next time, we told ourselves, we would chop it down and leave it to dry out. We never did have our log boat.

4. Friendship, Love and Growing Up

I ne'er was struck before that hour
With love so sudden and so sweet,
Her face it bloomed like a sweet flower
And stole my heart away complete.

John Clare.

The village green, the centre of our lives, where we grew up together, fell out, made friends again and later kissed and cuddled and touched and explored one another's bodies as we discovered our sexuality, and where we later said our departing goodbyes, is now lifeless.

On a recent visit there I was challenged by the house-owner of the house I once knew almost as well as the one I lived in and asked what I was doing. She knew nothing of the village, its history and its Roman origins or how it had got its name; of Vizziker or the names of the families that had lived there for generations. She didn't know that her front path was an ancient right of way which once had a stile over her wall and into the meadow beyond.

Her house had been where my first girlfriend with her flaming frizz of ginger hair and freckled face, three days my junior, had been born and lived. Our mothers were friends and we held hands on our first day at school. The day after she moved from the village I stood outside the house, unable to believe I would never see her again. I believe I was about seven years old. It was my first experience of real bereavement and the feeling of permanent loss of something precious. How could someone I had known all my life, my special friend, almost a twin, suddenly not be there anymore?

We children were very close, almost like an extended family as we shared growing up together. Their grans and aunties were our grans and aunties. Old ladies were always Granny this or Gran that; Gran Scarrott, Granny Crockford, Granny Ayres…We knew their houses almost as well as we knew our own. We didn't even knock at the door when we went in – they were never locked!

Some of my earliest recollections are of playing on The Green, mostly with girls of about my age because there were few other boys. There were only two of my age; both lived too far away from The Green to come there to play regularly. I believe my earliest recollection is of going into our house with the girl from next door and seeing my grandfather peeling potatoes. He gave us each a slice of raw potato which he cut with the pocket knife he always used. He was peeling them in a white enamel tin bowl with a blue rim. He died when I was three, aged 84 years old.

I remember the commotion when my mother found him lying on the garden where he had gone to cut a cabbage. His body was carried in by several men including my father and laid out in the front room. On the day of his funeral I had my first ride in a motor vehicle as our mother's brother, Uncle Jack, gave us a lift to the church in Finstock

There were just three boys near my age but my best friend was about four years older than me. One friend lived too far away to join in much until he (and his sister) was older. There were five girls of about that age. Most of us of the 'Boomer' generation had been born between1946 and 1948 as soldiers returning to their wives from the war celebrated with a new baby or two.

We 'Boomers' were to benefit not just from a brand new National Health Service but from new schools and services which had to be built to accommodate us. We grew up in the post-war economic boom and became the first teenagers to have a disposable income with which to buy the pop music of the 1960s and the last generation to have spent a large part of childhood without a television, a family car or the expectation of holidays and foreign travel.

We were the first rickets-free generation with free school milk for every child. We were probably the first generation of village children to never know real, malnourishing hunger, with cheap school dinners. Free National Heath orange juice and cod-liver oil gave us the vitamins to grow straight and strong and soon the Salk vaccine would free our parents from the fear of polio that had been the dread of earlier generations. Good clean drinking water had ended the regular epidemics of cholera that had filled the graveyards with young bodies in earlier generations and soon tuberculosis too would be a thing of the past.

This was a kind, caring society determined to build a better future for their children than their parents and grandparents had had, and the nation prospered. Soldiers came home fresh from victory aware of having helped put an end to something uniquely evil. They and the people who had survived the deprivation and destruction of war were determined to 'win the peace' too. They voted for a government through which Beveridge was to put an end to the 'five great evils' of squalor, ignorance, want, idleness, and disease, and they considered it worth paying more taxes to achieve it. Unashamedly Keynesian economics built a prosperous, housed, healthy and educated society.

One girl I had been brought up with was just two months younger than me. We went through school together, walking the mile and a half back from Finstock School four days a week together for six years. In many ways she had been the 'mother' of the group, looking after the younger ones on our way home and ushering them onto the grass verge when a lorry or car came along the footpath-free road; a wise and sensible head on very young shoulders. She was eleven when she had to take her neighbour's five year-old son behind a hedge to clean him up with leaves as best she could when he had had an unfortunate accident on the way home from school. She complained and swore like a fishwife but she did her duty!

Although I don't think she ever knew it, I thought she was beautiful with sallow skin, brown eyes and brown curls. To me, she epitomised 'beauty'. I would certainly never have had the courage to tell her. On one occasion when we are probably about twelve we had been playing tag and I had caught her. For some reason I stood with my hand round her shoulders for several minutes, almost subconsciously not wanting to let go and nor did she pull away but put her arm round my waste. We stood with our bodies against one another with my arm round her shoulders and my hand cupping the top of her arm, and her arm round my waist, until someone gave us a funny look, I felt embarrassed and she turned quickly away.

I hadn't really realised I was holding her; I just knew it felt good to have her close. I still remember looking at her and thinking how beautiful her skin was and how nicely she smelled! Soft and warm! And she was a girl! This was a new feeling for someone I had known since babyhood and who had been my country dance partner at the school Christmas concert when we were about ten, when holding sweaty hands was obligatory and part of the dance.

I kissed her for the first and last time the day before, aged sixteen and heavily pregnant, she married her boyfriend and left the village. We had travelled back from Oxford on the same bus that Friday evening, probably in about November, maybe later, and I walked down the dark lane with her to the green where she lived. I wished her luck and said I would miss her, and then we kissed on the mouth firmly but quickly and shyly and parted. I have never seen her again.

I went home and sobbed in the privacy of my bedroom as much for the thought of a lost love and another childhood friend gone, as for the thought that she was maybe being forced into a marriage she didn't want because there were no alternatives. I don't know if that was true – for all I know she has had a long and happy marriage – but a sixteen year-old unmarried mother was almost unthinkable in 1963 and a termination was illegal. Marriage for her would have been almost compulsory; she would have had very little choice. It was considered better for her to live with her young husband, taking their chances in life, than to remain in the safety of her family bringing up a child that would be forever branded as 'illegitimate'; a 'bastard'.

What a hideous society that can pin such a pejorative label on a child for the 'sin' of being born! With little in the way of effective contraception or sex education, even when we were becoming sexually liberated, a girl still 'had to get married' if she got pregnant – and very many did.

Later that evening I was with my girlfriend (not from Fawler) but I was thinking of someone else and wishing it could have been her. Her pregnant body pressed briefly against me and that brief kiss had been a real turn-on. But I loved my girlfriend no less for that, or I thought I did. It was not until some years later that I understood that love was more than sex and that there were far more ways to love a person than to have sex with them and far more ways for them to show they loved you than to give in to your demands. Unfortunately, I think a lot of girls, as well as a lot of boys thought love was lust and compliance. 'You would if you really loved me!' What did we know?

ooOoo

By that time Dad was working nights at the Radiators in Oxford. If I timed it right I could get home have dinner and get changed in the time it took Dad to go to Finstock and pick up a work mate. He picked me up on the way back through Fawler and dropped me off at Daphne and

Sheila's house in Stonesfield. Dad always said the same thing: "Behave yourself and don't be late home, and keep away from the pubs!"

Of course I never did. The Black Head pub was the place where we all met. There would be boys and girls from Woodstock, Long Hanborough or Bladon. I had lost weight, dyed my hair peroxide blond and discovered boys.

But still no sex! The pill was still in the early stages and not easily available and only given to married women. For me, fear of Dad was the best form of contraception. I was scared of what he would say. Mum used to say the most precious thing you can give your husband is your virginity, and I believed her. Morals were still high in the sixties.

The youth club movement was very strong in those days and we were all members. If we weren't at the Stonesfield Club then we had all piled into a car and gone to another one somewhere. I was always back in Stonesfield to catch the last bus home at 11 o'clock.

Every Friday and Saturday night there would be a disco, or a dance with live music, in one of the local villages. But living in Fawler I had a job to get anywhere, so Dad, bless him, took me to the dances and pick me up again at 11:45. If I had met a boy that night I had to say good night to him in the dance hall. Once I made the mistake of giving a kiss to a boy outside the hall. Dad wanted to know his name, where he came from, what he did for a living and who his parents were. I soon learnt that what he didn't know didn't hurt him. After a while I had a good circle of friends and if I hadn't met someone with a car to take me home I could always bank on one of the other boys giving me a lift.

ooOoo

Sex for us was like being a little bit naughty. Not really to be avoided, just got away with, like eating that cream cake you know you shouldn't eat, but you do anyway because it feels good. We didn't think of it as wrong, just something the grown-ups didn't want us to do even though they did it themselves – like smoking and drinking, and eating cream cakes. How could something that felt so natural and so right be wrong?

Why was it naughty to touch one another and look at one another's 'private' parts? It wasn't, of course, not for us as that age. It wasn't as though we hadn't seen them before! We were curious and sexual and had as childhood friends only a few years earlier been naked in front of one another as we changed on the river bank in all innocence, even peeing unashamedly in front of one another when the need arose. Had we not played doctors and nurses together even before we started school? Was there a Fawler girl of my age who hadn't shown me hers if I showed her mine? No, there wasn't!

We were crude and unsophisticated people who had no shame in our bodily functions, so we had few personal secrets. Now our bodies were changing and becoming more interesting. New and enticing scents were coming from them; strange urges were being felt and we wanted to try out the curiously exciting things we had been told about by the older children. Everything seemed to fit nicely into the palm of a hand and was begging to be stroked, twiddled and fondled. We wanted to taste one another, to put our mouths and tongues and fingers where we had never put them before.

Who was going to convince a fifteen year-old boy and his fourteen year-old girl that they shouldn't be making love in the long grass or on the riverbank or against a tree, and wanting to do it as often as possible? Could there be anything in the world more pleasurable than full and vigorous sex? What more endearing expression of love is there than the words, "Do it to me again like you did it yesterday!"?

What's the only thing better than one ice-cream? Two ice-creams of course, and ice-cream again tomorrow and maybe ice-cream with a different sauce!

The idea of the age of consent was only vaguely meaningful to us. The important consent was the consent of the girl. If she wanted it she was entitled to it and why should the law say she couldn't have it? When my girlfriend turned sixteen it suddenly all became legal but it didn't feel the slightest bit different. What had changed when the clock turned midnight? Nothing at all, of course! We still had to be careful not to get caught and to pretend to our parents we were just good friends and that we never did more than hold hands and kiss.

We all, even our parents, understood the taboo not so much of sex but of acknowledging that we were doing it; of talking about it. We did not talk about sex to adults, least of all to our parents unless they were especially enlightened. Officially, we knew nothing of sex! We were even shooed away when a cow was calving in case we got ideas or asked awkward questions.

One of my school friends was in a relationship with a fourteen year-old when we were fifteen and she talked openly of discussing sex with her parents who were, so she claimed, quite happy with her to sleep with him provided they were 'careful' and she told them about it. This was almost unbelievable to us and we were never sure if it was true or not, or just her being revolutionary and sophisticated.

We knew little of STDs or of effective contraception. It was almost impossible to buy condoms at that age and even if he had the half-crown needed, no fifteen year-old boy was going to buy a pack of three from the chemist or ask the barber for 'something for the weekend'. He would very likely tell your father!

When we managed to get them, condoms were toys. It meant sex was relaxed and worry-free and almost guaranteed. Having a condom in your pocket was like an aphrodisiac to a girl, or at least to my girl. It was like free sex and you could 'go all the way' without worry or guilt!

We poured over 'health' books if we could get them – there were none in the school library but my girlfriend's mother had one secreted in her bedroom (the slut!) – looking for information about safe periods so we knew when it was safe to 'take a risk'. Some of it was barely comprehensible so that at one point we believed the safe period was mid-way between her 'monthlies', believing, for some reason that the 'danger time' was just before and just after her period. Somehow we had managed to get it almost exactly wrong! And we were trying to be responsible!

Each month brought that flood of relief as she said she had 'started', even phoning me at work with the good news. Two days late seemed like an eternity, but still the risk was worth it. Somehow we got away with it and undeterred, took the same risks again next month.

We learned a tremendous amount together and the sex really was good for both of us for the most part, but our lives went in different directions and we ended up parting on not very good terms. We had been together for two and a half years and were bored with one another. My life had moved on. I now had friends and other interests in Oxford and I no longer wanted her. We were probably very lucky that we had not 'had to get married'.

I think about her often and hope she was and is happy. She was a sweet girl who just wanted to be loved and thought her very female body was all she had to offer. Sadly, it was all I wanted too, and I accepted it gladly. I also thought my body was all I had to give and loved that she wanted it as much as I wanted hers. I had no idea about low self-esteem and how I was exploiting her need to be loved. I mistook it for love for me and probably so did she.

Sex education in 1961 was non-existent. For most people it was a taboo subject within the family, so we had no other sources of information other than what we learned from the older children. Myths were rife about how a girl could or couldn't get pregnant – doing it standing up was safer than laying down but it was safer still if she jumped up and down or went for a run afterwards. We believed wrongly that a bottle of gin drunk in a hot bath would get rid of an unwanted pregnancy safely and legally, as would eating a whole grated nutmeg.

We boys believed that we only had to touch a girl's breasts or touch her between her legs or get her to touch our penis for her to become aroused and uncontrollable with passion, so seduction was a hand inside her knickers or inside her blouse, and a lot of fumbling. If you got the bra off you were half-way there. If you got her knickers down you were probably there! Oh! Happy the day she told you she wasn't wearing any, if you hadn't discovered that already! "Oh! You've got your fur knickers on today!" Nudge, nudge!

If you got close and she still wouldn't do it this was because she didn't love you or she was 'frigid'. It was always her fault! Moral blackmail was the seduction of choice followed by a lot of sulking and guilt projection if that didn't work. Unfortunately, a lot of girls seemed to believe that was how it worked too. To keep a boy, you had to let him have his way to show him you loved him. Girls were never taught to expect more or to feel entitled to more from a relationship. What did we know about making a girl feel valued and appreciated for her mind as well as her body?

It was a misogynistic society and few people questioned the rightness of it. The 'weaker sex' was assumed even by themselves, to be inferior to men and entitled to nothing more than being a man's wife, never his equal. It was what they were for.

Our education specifically moulded us for our roles with girls doing needlework and cookery and boys doing carpentry and gardening.

Other classes were divided down the middle with boys on one side and girls on the other. Several teachers directed the lesson at the boys while the girls looked on, usually in disinterest. I remember one maths teacher who barely acknowledged the presence of the girls, telling one girl that she didn't need maths to have babies and do housework!

Women were to get married and to be their husband's domestic servants, their cooks, their children's nannies and their sex toys. They routinely left work when they married because they were expected to devote their time to looking after their husband, and his children and cooking and cleaning for him. It was a woman's ordained role and what marriage was for. The Bible and the church were in no doubt about that at all. The man was master of his household and that was the natural and proper order of things.

The police were reluctant to intervene in domestic violence because it was a 'private matter' between husband and wife. It had not been long since a woman literally handed over all her worldly goods to her husband on marriage and had nothing save what he gave her. A wife almost literally became the possession of her husband and had no legal separate identity. She could not even bring a case of assault against him because she could not testify in law against him, having promised to 'obey' him in her marriage vows. A husband was legally entitled to beat his wife provided the rod was no thicker than his thumb!

She could not legally refuse her husband sex so there was no offence of rape within a marriage. A woman's body was not her own but her husband's plaything. If he 'had' to force himself on her then **she** was at fault for not being a dutiful wife and not keeping to her marriage vows. You couldn't expect a man to control his urges and accept 'no' for an answer. He had 'conjugal rights'!

Although the law had been changed a little it still had a long way to go in 1961 and the social attitudes that underpinned this institutionalised misogyny were still very much in evidence. The 'Boomer' generation was to change all that or at least put society on a course which would eventually reject much of the old Bible-based division and discrimination and start to treat women as full members of the human race.

Maybe a measure of the way things were changing privately if not publicly was in the attitude to virginity. There had been a general assumption up to maybe the early 1960s that it was desirable for a girl to be a virgin. Maybe not waiting until she was married but certainly until things became 'serious' with the man she was eventually to marry. A promiscuous girl – a girl of easy virtue – was a not a good girl. By the mid–1960s attitudes had changed to the extent that girls would be reluctant to admit they were virgins! By the age of seventeen or eighteen we expected our friends to be sexually active, even sex–obsessed. A 'good girl' was now one who didn't have sex on the first date but managed to resist temptation until the second or third date.

Sex was still clandestine however; it was to be another generation before teenagers began to bring their boyfriends and girlfriends home to spend the night with them.

5. To Everything There Is a Season

Sweet scene of my youth!
Seat of Friendship and Truth,
Where Love chas'd each fast-fleeting year
Loth to leave thee, I mourn'd,
For a last look I turn'd,
But thy spire was scarce seen through a Tear:

Lord Byron

To a rural agricultural community the turning of the seasons absolutely dictates the pace of life. Although my family weren't farmworkers, my grandfather had been a shepherd and most of our friends' families worked on the local farm and many lived in the tied farm–workers' cottages. To me, there was always something to look forward to as the seasons turned but probably the thing I looked forward to the most, like all children, was Christmas.

But before Christmas was another event between the end of the summer holidays and the Christmas holidays – Bonfire Night – probably the biggest social event of the year when just about all the families gathered together on the village green to watch the bonfire and set off fireworks.

Preparation for Bonfire Night started in the last two weeks of the summer holidays when we started to make the bonfire. If we were lucky there would be a large elm tree down or a large branch fallen somewhere close by so we could cut the 'brushwood' out and drag it back to the green. If not, we cut branches off the sycamores which grew like weeds in the hedges.

The old double hedge that was once 'Vizziker' that headed off towards the old slate pits was the favourite. This led down to the 'nuttery' – a piece of rough grassland too stony to plough and probably the overgrown site of old earthworks of unknown age. Here we could cut down suitable brushwood without making a hole in a hedge which had a good, stock-proof fence on the pasture side anyway.

All the children were expected to take part and do their bit. It was a status thing that the bigger children pulled bigger bundles, roped together. If we had a really big branch maybe two of us would pull it together. One year a particularly large elm on the far side of the water-meadow shed a very large bough. We descended on it with glee as did some of the women of the village. Armed with saws and axes we hacked off the brush-wood and dragged it back across the meadow, making a visible track and piled it up to make the bonfire on the green.

We sawed off logs as large as we could carry or put in old prams, handcarts and wheelbarrows to take back home for firewood. Some of us had 'trackers' made from old pram wheels and any old wood we could find. These were pressed into use to cart as much firewood home as we could manage. Nothing went to waste. Sawn up on sawing horses and split into blocks for the fire these would go a long way to supplementing the winter fuel. There is something satisfying about putting a block of wood on the fire and watching it hiss and spurt steam as the remaining sap boils off. Green elm would burn slowly but it didn't spit and pop and throw sparks onto the hearth rug like pine does.

So, by the time we went back to school at the end of the summer holiday we had a sizeable pile of brushwood for the November bonfire. Apart from asking Wally Scarrott, the local shop-keeper and baker, to save up his empty boxes for us, we did little more to the bonfire until a couple of weeks before bonfire night, when work would start in earnest again.

The large horse chestnut tree, a feature of The Cross and under which we would shelter from the rain when waiting for a bus, would obligingly shed all its leaves over a couple of days just before Bonfire Night. These were gathered up by the sack–full or heaped into wheelbarrows and carts to be piled up around the base of the bonfire. We hoped it would stay dry so the bonfire would burn quickly with a good blaze and not 'smoulder' sullenly come the big night!

Wally Scarrott's empty cardboard boxes were added on the last day just in case it rained. If we were lucky, someone would procure a bale or two of straw to be broken up and pushed well into the base just before it was lit.

Just before that the 'Guy' had been placed on top. The Guy was made from an old coat and trousers stuffed with paper. The Guy's head was usually a stuffed paper bag with a stick rammed down the neck of the coat and a face drawn on the back of a piece of card cut from a cereal box. The important thing was that it had a pointed beard and a bristling moustache drawn on it!

For some reason my family traditionally made the Guy, or at least it was made in our 'hovel' – the lean-to fuel shed attached to the end of our house. I don't know why or whether this was just something we had taken upon ourselves but we jealously guarded the privilege. There seemed to be an important principle involved but one year someone made another one and the bonfire had two Guys.

No-one seemed to have thought of health and safety. We bought penny bangers, jumping jacks and thru'penny rockets from Wally Scarrott's shop for weeks before bonfire night and treated them like toys. We made hand-held rocket launchers out of bamboo and cotton reels; we made flaming torches out of old golden syrup or cocoa tins nailed to the end of sticks and filled with paraffin-soaked rags. We stuck bangers in the ground, lit then and put a jar or a milk bottle over them before they went off, to see how high it would go. We even tied bangers to rockets to try to make them explode in the air, but they usually nose-dived because the added weight was too much.

And so, come November 5th, almost the whole village came together to stand round the bonfire and let off their fireworks. Towards the end of the evening the unburned wood would be pushed into the middle of the heap of red-hot ash and we went home tired but happy, congratulating ourselves on what a great bonfire we had made again.

The next day we would collect up the old fireworks and throw them into the still hot and maybe still burning remains of the bonfire to see if they would have a little spark left. The blackened soil and the ash would stay there until next year. I don't know for how long Fawler people had been building a bonfire on that spot but it was certainly for many years before our Boomer generation.

Later on, when the area of rough ground had been fenced off and turned into a playground, the bonfire moved to a different part of the green.

The playground is now gone and seems to have been bought and turned into a private paddock. The other part of the village green is planted with daffodils in a parody of what someone thinks a village green should be. A weeping willow which was planted there about ten years ago has mercifully been removed. Frankly, I'm surprised someone hasn't put a little wishing well on The Green or planted a spreading chestnut tree 'neath which a village smithy stands. Was that too cynical? Maybe.

There is no longer an annual bonfire, no annual gathering of the families, no collective effort by the children. The once rough grass; home to slowworms, grasshoppers, butterflies, beetles by the hundred, a couple of ancient white ant 'hills' and the occasional hawkmoth caterpillar on the ladies bedstraw is gone. Where I once released my paint–numbered 'Roman' snails to see how far they would go, is now neatly mowed and looks just like the village green from a child's picture book.

And it is just as lifeless.

Bonfire night over, it was all downhill to Christmas. Christmas was a day of unbridled joy and happiness. What could be more perfect than a pillowcase full of new toys and smelling of that heady scent of new cardboard, oranges and nuts! You could stick your head in your

Christmas pillowcase and smell love and security and know that you had been good enough to deserve presents from Santa again!

Christmas had started weeks earlier as we planned for it well in advance. As well as busying ourselves with making Christmas presents for our parents and decorations for the tree at school, Finstock School children had the school concert to rehearse and get ready for. We had to learn songs and country dances and little plays and we even had a 'dress rehearsal' in the village hall a few days before the big night. Not for us a simple nativity scene! This was to be a virtual pantomime!

I was in the country dance team and once sung the male solo in one of the folk songs we sang. For some reason the back row in the choir stood on 'forms' – the long, folding benches we sat on at dinner time. Woe-betide the boy who made it wobble! That would probably mean a cane across both hands!

Backstage, come the night – actually the side room and kitchen – was a hysterical frenzy of half–naked children getting changed and trying not to tear their crepe paper costumes, or searching for that plimsoll that someone had kicked under a bench, and increasingly irate teachers. But somehow the show went on, the right record was put on the wind-up gramophone for the right country dance and the choir managed to come in together on the third beat. How we managed that whilst frantically searching the audience in semi-darkness to see if our parents had remembered to turn up was anyone's guess.

And only a little prompting was needed when lines were forgotten or someone said their lines in the wrong place and started to cry.

The important thing was that we got to the end and the audience clapped. It would have been the worst thing imaginable if they hadn't clapped, but they always did so we had obviously been good and no one had noticed the odd mistake.

I was very proud one year when my normal country dance partner wasn't well and my secret favourite Fawler girl replaced her even though she didn't know the sequence of steps. "I'll tell you", I said, and I did very quietly and with hand signals. She followed my lead and danced perfectly! Never a step wrong and no-one even noticed! How proud I was! And how beautiful she looked – but I wasn't going to tell her. She became my regular country dance partner from then on because she 'liked dancing with me', so she said.

And soon it was Christmas. For a proper Christmas holly was essential. I knew which holly trees would have berries, so my job was to get the holly a few days before. Some years this was easy because there were plenty of berries; other years they were few and far between and we might have to settle for just a few berries and a lot of green leaves, but this wasn't a job to be shirked! If there were berries to be had I would find them! Well, what's the point of knowing every tree in the woods if you can't find holly berries when you need them?

It would be easy and a great sentimental pleasure to describe Christmas Day as we experienced it, but our Christmas may not have been typical; indeed it definitely wasn't typical for some families. Each family probably had its own traditions, some like ours and some quite different. Christmas being a family occasion it was also in some ways a private occasion since we tended to spend the entire day ensconced in our own homes with our own families doing what we always did.

But Christmas was a time of good cheer and good fellowship; a time for neighbourliness and a time to be grateful for what we had. Old enmities were put aside for a day as we wished everyone we saw, "Merry Christmas!"

I'll leave my sister Patricia to record her very poignant memory of a Hounslow Family Christmas:

ooOoo

Christmas was one of the best times of the year. It was magical.

Weeks before Christmas Mum made the Christmas puddings, mixing all the dry ingredients together the night before. I can remember picking at the dried fruit in the large mixing bowl. I always tried to find the dates; they were my favourite. The next day all the other ingredients were added and we all had to stir the pudding and make a wish. We weren't allowed to say what we had wished for or it wouldn't come true. The mixture was then put in several pudding bowls and covered with greaseproof paper then a pudding cloth tied round with string. These were put into a saucepan of boiling water and boiled for hours. Every so often Mum checked them to make sure the pan hadn't boiled dry.

The cloth and paper were then removed and a fresh piece of greaseproof paper over the basin and tied round with string to seal it. The puddings were stored on the shelf with all the jams and bottled fruit.

At school, we would be busy making Christmas cards, calendars, paper–chains and paper lanterns, snow men and Father Christmas's, all made out of card, cotton wool and glitter...

All I can say about Christmas Eve is "magical!" Aunty Milly had arrived and was seated in a chair by the roaring tire. Mum was in the kitchen making mince pies, sausage rolls, Christmas biscuits – iced pink and white with hundreds and thousands shaken over – and stuffing for the goose. Aunty Milly beat the butter, icing sugar and brandy together to make the brandy butter. A large piece of gammon was boiling away on the cooker. Everything smelled of "Christmas".

We kids could hardly contain ourselves. There would be Mickey Mouse cartoons on the telly, with Donald Duck and Goofy and the Chipmunks causing chaos; sometimes a Lassie film. We loved them as we had never seen anything like it. It was all so new. No colour telly, it was all in black and white.

The last minute wrapping had been done, using last year's wrapping paper and silver, red or gold glitter string. Nothing was wasted. The paper had been ironed and folded and put away last year as it would be again this year. No labels, you just wrote the person's name on the wrapper, so each year you scribbled one name out before you wrote another. Recycling was natural then; you had to. You couldn't afford not to.

If the radio was on it played carols and Christmas songs. "Mary's Boy Child", "Little Donkey", "White Christmas", "When Santa Got Stuck up the Chimney", were but a few.

I can't remember what we had for tea at night. Nothing much because Mum was too busy preparing things for the next day. I don't think we could eat that much anyway; we were far too excited.

After tea was the best. The candles were lit on the tree. Dad spent ages checking to make sure there wasn't a branch too close that could catch fire. All the lights went out and we sat and sang carols and songs. With just the candle light and the fire light it was wonderful. It truly was a holy night. There was always talk of how at midnight all the animals could talk. We so badly wanted to stay up to see if the cats could talk to us. As Children, we never went to church, but at times like that it felt as if God was in the room with us.

So to bed, but first it was up to the lavatory at the top of the garden, stopping on the way and looking up into the sky to see if the star of

Bethlehem had appeared, and a quick glance on the way back to try and see Father Christmas flying through the sky in his sledge.

Mary and Lilian were much older than Bill, Chris and me, so could stay up later. We were each given a pillow–case which was laid carefully at the bottom of the bed. Then into bed we jumped and closing our eyes tight we tried desperately to go to sleep, because Father Christmas "won't come if you are awake".

But oh, we couldn't, we giggled and talk so much that Mum had to shout at us from the bottom of the stairs to be quiet and go to sleep. We then used to lay still and try and stay awake so we could catch a glimpse of him. Of course the next thing we knew we woke up and could feel the pillow–case stuffed full of presents at the bottom of the bed. Shouts of "He's been!" made sure everyone was awake.

If it was too early, Mum tried to make us stay in bed a bit longer. We were not allowed to open our presents until everyone was up and in Mum's and Dad's room. So if we had to wait, then we felt the presents to see if we could tell what was inside. At the bottom of the pillow–case was a large orange, a sugar mouse and a bag of chocolate coins.

At long last it was time, and carrying our pillow–cases we went down the attic stairs and into Mum's and Dad's bedroom. Then it was a mad flurry and shrieks and squeals of delight as one by one our presents were opened. Mum trying to tell us to open them carefully so she could see who had given us what so we could thank them for it and also so she could use the paper again. Their bed was covered in Christmas paper, string, toys, books and new slippers. The next thing we did was to go along the landing to Aunty Milly's room to show her what we had been given. I don't know why she never came into Mum's and Dad's room with us but perhaps she found it too noisy.

Then we went down stairs to see what presents had been left on the tree, straining our necks trying to find them in between the branches. We never opened these presents until after Dinner.

Cups of tea were made by Mary or Lilian and taken up to Mum and Dad and Aunty Milly.

After a breakfast of boiled eggs and cold gammon we played with our new toys. Chris and I always had similar; a dolly with hand knitted clothes, an annual from our favourite comic, a new hand knitted jumper or cardigan, paints and colouring books and, my favourite, a book of cut out dolls all with different outfits to dress them in. I remember one year having a cardboard model of the Queen's play house. I kept it for years, only playing with it occasionally. I'm not sure what happened to it but I expect it finally got so tatty it was thrown away.

Aunty Ivy always sent us a present, usually a hand bag each. Inside the handbag was a sixpenny piece. It was considered unlucky to give a handbag as a present without putting some money inside it. Aunty Ivy was Mum's cousin and lived in Oxford with Uncle Bill.

Bill had things like Meccano, model aeroplanes and chocolate smoking sets. I really can't remember what Lilian and Mary had, but Mum always had the calendars we had made at school and some soap and a new brooch or necklace. Poor Dad always had socks, razors, hankies and a cigar to smoke after dinner.

One year Chris gave Mum a penny, a half-penny and a threepenny bit all wrapped up in Christmas paper. Mum said it was the best present she had ever had, as Chris had given her all she had. Mum has still got the coins in a little box on her dressing table.

At eleven o'clock Dad opened a bottle of sherry. He had been bought up tea–total so alcohol was only drunk in small quantities on very special occasions. A toast was said to wish us all a very happy Christmas. We younger kids were only allowed lemonade.

At one o'clock lunch was served. The goose was done to perfection. There were mountains of roast and mashed potatoes, Brussels–sprouts, carrots and peas. Dad carved the goose along with a slice of sausage meat and stuffing. Mum dished up the vegetables, and gravy.

After the first course Mum marched in with the pudding held high. Even if you were full up you still found room for a little slice because hidden in the pudding was a sixpence. Feeling it in your mouth, and sucking the fruit and brandy butter off, before holding it high with shouts of "I've found it!" caused great fun and excitement. Dad somehow always managed to find half–crown in his pudding, making a great to do about it nearly breaking his false teeth. There was always a plate of warm mince pies on the table but nobody ever had room to eat one.

The washing up took ages; kettle after kettle of hot water with Mum washing up and Dad and all us kids wiping up. The relief after it was finished was made the better with a welcome cup of tea, all laid out on a tray with tea pot, milk jug and sugar bowl. A box of Milk Tray chocolates was opened and handed round, just in time for the Queen's speech. We dare not make a noise, and we hung on every word she said.

When the national anthem was played Dad stood up to attention, and we all followed his example. No laughing or thinking Dad odd. He had fought long and hard in the war and this must have been his way of showing how proud he was of this country. It was the same when we got older and he took us to the pictures. At the end of the film the National Anthem was always played. Dad stood to attention and wouldn't move until it had finished, but then so did most of the other people as well.

This was the time the tree presents were opened; maybe some bubble–bath a puzzle or if we had had a doll as a present another set of clothes had been knitted to fit her.

Mum and Dad then tried to have a little sleep. Looking back they must have been exhausted but never a cross word.

And then tea...

[Tea consisted of] cold goose and ham sandwiches, some with mustard and some without, sausage rolls, pickled onions, jelly and blancmange with tinned Nestlé's cream, a huge home–made Christmas cake iced like a snow scene and decorated with a father Christmas, a snowman, a deer and some holly. Again, as with Christmas decorations, the same few used every year; so much so that they became old friends. I've still got them and use them myself.

[There would also be] a chocolate log with a robin and a piece of holly as decoration. This was always bought from Mr. Scarrott's shop.

[We had] Christmas crackers and indoor fireworks placed on a tin plate and, when set alight, either burned into the shape of a snake or made pretty coloured smoke.

Set to one side was a cardboard figure of a Father Christmas or a snowman and when opened from underneath revealed small presents for everybody, only small, maybe a comb or hair slide a small pack of cards or a whistle.

And then the washing up again...

The evening was spent singing songs round the candle–lit tree, each one of us doing a "turn", and playing games such as spin the plate.

Again we all had a drink; Mum had a gin and orange, Bill and Dad a shandy and Aunty Milly a small sherry. As a treat, Chris and I were allowed a tiny drop of port mixed with lemonade. We thought this was wonderful. We had great fun pretending we were drunk. Drink was only bought at Christmas.

Supper, if we had room, was let over sandwiches, sausage rolls and mince pies.

Bed time came all too soon. But we went to bed very full and very happy.

ooOoo

And Christmas was over for another year. The decorations stayed up until Twelfth Night, of course but now we had winter snow, tobogganing and sliding on the frozen floods to look forward to before going back to school. It always seemed to snow in winter. It even used to snow before Christmas in some years. And there were always frosts. I don't remember ever going through a winter as a child and not having at least one good snowstorm which blanketed the land.

Snow, when it came, covered the countryside in a deep, white blanket and. if there had been any drifting, often closed the roads for a day or two until the drifts had either thawed or been dug through. Wonderful shapes would appear along the hedgerows as drifting snow carved out amazing waves and curves and organic-looking sculptures that glistened in the sun. Wonderful animal tracks would appear in the fields.

The tracks of hares, rabbits, voles, birds and even foxes could be seen on a walk across the fields. One Christmas I had a book about nature which had all these tracks in it so I felt I was an expert! The bird tracks would end in a beautiful wing print as the pigeon or pheasant, crow or duck took off.

Little patches of snow would be strangely yellow and we quickly learned not to eat yellow snow. We quickly learned to make our own yellow patches too, and even to write our names in the snow – something to show off about to the girls, who lacked that ability just as they lacked the ability to pee up a wall. They were so unlucky, being girls and not being able to do the things any boy could do!

For a few years, maybe only two, we had a sledge made from fence railings, a spar across the front end for our feet, or hands if we laid down on it, and a wooden board to sit or lay on. If the snow wasn't too deep this went like a rocket, jumping over the jumps half way down the hill, made by a natural sudden increase in the slope of the hill. The further along the hill we went, the steeper it became and the shaper the jump. But, it was further and steeper to pull the sledge back up.

If the snow was too deep, we would scrape out a track with walls of snow built up at the sides. We even tried to make curved tracks to see if we could get the sledge to follow them. It was a real skill to jerk the sledge to make it turn, or to lean over onto one runner or the other to get it to change direction. Mostly, we were at the mercy of the sledge and just hung on till it stopped, or dug into an ant or mole hill with one runner and spun round throwing you off into the snow.

When we got bored with sledging and our arms and legs ached from pulling the sledge back up the hill, we would make igloos, or giant snowballs by rolling a ball of snow around until it was too big to roll or it fell apart. We left the hillside littered with sledge tracks, igloos (often without the roof on because it kept fall in, and giant snowballs that would still be there days after the rest of the snow has melted.

The late afternoons on the snow-covered hillside were often bitterly cold so our faces stung with the cold as the sun sank, casting a pink-golden glow across the field. If the snow came again it would drive stingingly into our faces, but even a driving blizzard was no reason to go home. Scarves, gabardine macs, maybe an old army balaclava, and a

pair of woollen gloves would be enough. But gloves were such a nuisance! You couldn't make a decent snowball and they got wet and made your hands even colder!

Two pairs of socks, usually soaked from all the snow that had gone down our wellies, and often screwed up in the toe because your wellies seemed to take your socks off, were enough to keep us warm enough if we ran around and tucked our hands up into our armpits or shook them vigorously and clapped to warm them up. Snow was too good to waste by going home just because your hands, feet and ears hurt from the cold.

We dreaded the words 'a general thaw', which meant our playground would be gone in a day or two. Rain was the worst possible thing because everything went cold and slushy. We would try to sledge with hardly any snow just so long as there was a little on the hillside and enough to get up enough speed to take us over the bare grass to the next patch of snow.

The winter of 1962–63 was something else. It deserves a special mention. It came almost as a punctuation mark for me as my life was about to change when I left school and entered the working class in Oxford.

I was the village's provider of Sunday newspapers! I felt I had an important job to do because without me no–one would have anything to read on Sunday mornings! It was a sacred duty to get the Sunday newspapers delivered!

So, on Sunday, 30th December 1962 I got up as usual to go to Charlbury to buy my 60 newspapers. I noticed there had been some snow and, unusually, the snow on the lower window frame on the back door seemed to be three or four inches up the glass.

I opened the door to go to the outside toilet. A pile of snow fell into the kitchen. The back yard was full of snow, literally.

I went out of the front door to find the world had changed beyond recognition! The Lane was full of snow! A snowdrift came straight off our garage roof, across the front garden, over the garden wall and up to the wall of the house opposite. It was deeper by far than my, by now, 5 feet 10 inches.

And the snow was still falling thick and fast, driven by a howling wind! Southern England was in the grip of a major blizzard not seen since 1947 and probably much earlier. Bitterly cold Arctic winds drove the dry, powdery snow into every hollow and piled it up until the hollow was full, then moved on to fill the next, deeper hollow, until the countryside was a smooth as plastered wall.

But the newspapers had to get through!

So, donning wellies with two pairs of thick socks, jumpers, overcoat, scarves – one over my head and over my mouth, another round my neck twice – a balaclava helmet and two pairs of gloves, I slung my paper sack over my shoulder and set out. It was a strange landscape but Main Road wasn't too deeply covered. There were no car tracks!

I trudged up through the village to just beyond the Finstock turn, marvelling at the deepening drifts, and even stopping to help a man trying to get his car out of his drive. It was there I met our neighbour's son-in-law walking over from Charlbury to check on her.

"You goin' to get yer papers?" he asked incredulously.

"Well, Dad can't drive me so I'm walkin'!" I explained.

"Well, turn round and go 'ome" he said. "No–one's goin' to get their papers today!"

"Is it that bad?"

"Corse it is! Even the trains ent runnin! Nothin's movin' anywhere."

So I turned round and went 'ome, and had a cup of hot soup made out of the remains of the Christmas goose. The village was totally shut off! For the first time on my watch, the Sunday newspapers had not been delivered.

We dug out the lane down to The Green so people could get to the shop but the shop couldn't get supplies in and was beginning to run down as a village shop anyway, as people got cars and could shop at the new supermarkets in Witney and Chipping Norton. The bakery had ceased to operate several years earlier.

It was a time for community action!

"If you can get your orders to the farm by 10 o'clock, one of the men will drive a tractor across the fields to the Co–op in Charlbury." We got our groceries delivered to the farm. We were told to collect all the free milk we wanted from the farm as the dairy cows still had to be milked but nothing could be got out. Churns of milk were simply poured away.

One council employee tried to keep the road between Fawler (and Finstock, so through to Witney) open with a mechanical digger but the road filled in behind him as he dug his way through. He spent most of one day just trying to open the road for a half–mile stretch where the snow blew down across flat fields to fill up the road to the level of the hedges either side. In the end, he gave up, cut a hole in the hedge at either end of the stretch and made a makeshift road across the field. Essential vehicles were towed across the field.

One local doctor did his house calls on skis.

The winter dragged on with perpetual frost day after day. Water pipes froze underground and tractor batteries were pressed into service to try to heat them up to thaw them out. Tea was made with boiled snow.

And I just had to get to Charlbury every evening to see my girlfriend! I walked through ice gorges with deeply rutted roads and saw wonderful meteor showers in the brilliantly clear sky. 1963 was not only to coldest but the sunniest winter on record.

Then we had the ice storm!

A blast of warm moist air hit the cold air over the snowfields of England and its water condensed out as what would have been torrential rain, only to freeze solid into frozen raindrops as it hit the cold air below and spread a thick crust of ice beads about two inches thick on top of the deep snow.

Then is snowed and snowed hard as another blizzard hit!

And the snow now had a smooth skating rink to blow across and every snowflake came pouring across the smooth fields and filled up the roads again, this time to the top of the ice gorge. I decided I was going to go to Charlbury that evening because I had a warm and cosy girlfriend waiting.

I reached the ice gorge to see a complete white blanket of snow pouring off the top of the drifts, swirling in the driving wind, so I put my head down and ran through it. It went on for a hundred yards or more and I emerged from the other side white with snow on my right–hand side, I wiped the snow off my face and hurried on.

My girlfriend's house had a lovely fire going and her brave hero had got through the blizzard. My wet coat was hanging to dry and my wellies were by the back door. And my right ear felt funny! I touched it. It was encased in ice! My ear was frozen! An ear–shaped piece of ice lay in my hand and within seconds bemusement turned to misery as it felt as though my ear was held in a vice! I fell to my knees almost screaming with pain for several minutes until the pain subsided and my ear turned a shade of crimson and throbbed.

The next day it looked like it had been shut in a vice as it went purple. I narrowly avoided frostbite but the edge of my ear pealed and became corrugated. It still is!

For a while the ice storm made walking over the drifts easier as it was thick enough to bear the weight of an adult, but walking was still treacherous as the slightest slope became a downward slide with nothing to stop you until you reached the bottom – whatever and wherever the bottom was.

Then it began to thaw briefly and the ice crust thinned and lost strength. It was a gamble now. Did you walk over the snowdrift on the ice and risk your foot suddenly going through up to your groin, leaving you to struggle out with a welly full of snow, often needing to crawl and with your other leg likely to go through too, or did you walk along the rutted and treacherous road (or what had been the road)?

Tobogganing became a lethal pastime! A toboggan would skim across the ice crust with no hope of control by dragging a foot in the snow to make it turn. It went downhill, gathering speed with almost no resistance until it either hit an uphill stretch or came to a natural stop after a half a mile or so. Using a toboggan on the hill over the downstream water meadow became dangerous as there was a serious risk of going right across the field into the river. The Evenlode was frozen over for the only time in living memory, but coming over the high bank on a toboggan was definitely to be avoided.

One of my school friends came to school one day with his face covered in lacerations. His toboggan had dug a runner into the snow throwing him face–first into the ice crust. "It was like going into a glass window", he explained.

1963 was 'O'–level year for us Spendlove School kids. We were the first Secondary School children to be allowed to stay on into the Fifth Form to take 'O'–levels and I had pleaded with my parents to let me stay on at school. There was no way I was going to miss any more school than I absolutely had to, so I walked.

On one occasion I walked through freezing fog, arriving with the front of my hair and the fur on my fur–collard coat white with hoarfrost, to discover that almost no–one else had turned up. We spent the morning in the assembly hall, had a 'school dinner' of bread and cheese, then went home. None of the school busses had run – which is why I walked in the first place.

And the winter went on.

Three months with frosts every night and a thaw never materialising until late March. When the snow finally went, the grass was yellow. The last to go was that piled up at the sides of the road where it had been since late December.

And during that winter we fell in love with the Beatles and Beatlemania gripped Britain and America. In 1963 British groups dominated the US charts and England began to swing. Life was good! I bought myself and my girlfriend a transistor radio and I had music as I walked over to Charlbury and back.

Gradually, winter gave way to spring. Primroses appeared in the woods and hedgerows and cowslips in the meadows, followed by violets along the roadside. What a delight, to see a mass of little purple violets set amongst their bright green leaves! Can there be any better symbol of spring? Oh what a heady scent too! To burry your nose deep into a bunch of freshly-picked violets is only bettered, if at all, by burying your nose into a bunch of freshly-picked primroses or cowslips. From as earlier as I could remember, I always took a bunch of flowers home to Mum if I found some.

Suddenly, the countryside seemed to wake up and sprout green everywhere. The hawthorns in the hedges and the cow parley on the roadside; the spathes of cuckoopint and annoyingly, the fresh shoots of stinging nettle which would soon shut us out of patches of countryside that we had been able to walk through in winter, burst forth in great profusion, giving the countryside a clean, freshly washed look.

Gathering food for my pet guinea-pig became a pleasure after the difficulty finding enough fresh grass in the winter, unless I left it too late and grabbed a handful of nettles in the dark.

And very soon there would be bird's nests in the hedges – blackbirds, linnets, thrushes, chaffinches, bullfinches, hedge-sparrows (as we called dunnocks), long-tailed tits, wrens and robins – all to be found if you knew where to look, and I knew where to look. I had a large collection of bird's eggs before I knew any better and before it became illegal. It is now illegal even to disturb a nesting bird but then, collecting bird's eggs was a respectable hobby for a boy. I had a strict code of honour though. I only ever took an egg if there was more than one (or else they might desert the nest) but less than a full clutch (because they might have started to incubate and there might be a chick in the egg).

I had most of the common bird's eggs, even a kestrel's, taken from a nest in the hole where an old elm had shed a bough. I even had a swan's egg, taken from a flooded nest when the river rose unexpectedly after a heavy rain. This was the first time swans had nested in this spot and they deserted the nest, never to return. So I had no guilt about taking the two eggs.

On the Evenlode, with their nests amongst the rushes, there were moorhens by the hundred and little grebes in places, more often heard but not seen as they plopped into the water to swim to safety under water. Mallards nested on the river bank in long grass or frequently on the platform formed at the top of the trunk of a pollard willow. I remember being incensed when I read in my authoritative book of

British Birds that mallards never nest in trees. They did and I could prove it! This trauma may be why I decided to question everything and be prepared to change my mind. Even the experts could be wrong!

We found jackdaws and owl nests in the larger holes in trees, starlings' nests in smaller holes, and of course the odd coal-tit and stock dove. Very occasionally we found a nest we could not identify by its eggs, so it was home to pour over the Observer's Book of Bird's Eggs until we found it. Not many eggs beat me as I just about knew the Observer's Book of Bird's Eggs and the Observer's Book of British Birds by heart. I wasn't very good on the coastal waders but there weren't many of those in rural Oxfordshire.

The fascinating thing to me was how nature and the countryside all seemed to mesh neatly together. The birds nested in the hedges just as the leaves were giving them cover and the new leaves then provided food for the caterpillars and other insects the birds needed for their young. In a good year, several species could get off two or even three clutches of eggs while the going was good. If a severe winter, when many small birds died, was followed by a decent spring and summer, the population could spring back in a single year.

A typical example of this is the wren which, in Britain is close to the northern limit of its range. The male wren's breeding strategy is to build lots of different nests then try to entice females to use as many of them as possible. If she chooses his nest he gets to mate with her. This means there are a lot of unused wren's nests which are used as collective roosts during the winter. In a very cold night the entire roost can be wiped out.

After the very hard winter of 1963 I found probably ten or a dozen wren's nests along the overhang at the top of an old shallow quarry face in the wood across the downstream water meadow. Each contained maybe half a dozen or more mummified bodies of wrens. Almost the entire population of that small wood must have perished in that winter but, within a year or two, the population was back to previous levels. The few survivors and those moving north into the area found little competition for food or nest sites, so the population rebounded.

Nature, red in tooth and claw, is uncaring and merciless and the only thing that matters is that there is a next generation. If there is not, the species goes extinct and nature cares not one jot.

It was the realisation that there must be a reason for this apparent organisation and rhythm and yet its uncaring, mercilessness, with suffering being an integral part of life, that started me to question the simplistic ideas we were fed at school and which seemed to explain everything so easily and so dismissively as little more than magic.

The magnificence of nature is too wonderful to be so easily dismissed as essentially a conjuring trick, and it just isn't kind, caring and benevolent. For most creatures, life is nasty, brutish and short and they get through it as best they can and normally die horribly. The cosy answer religion provides is a reason not to want to know; an easy answer which isn't bothered about the truth so long as it fits in with a preconceived idea.

I was too young to think in those terms as a child but I knew the answer wasn't simple and that it would be better and more interesting than the simple notions we were being told. Other questions were building up in my mind and demanding to be answered. They were, quite suddenly one day, as I will relate later.

In the middle of spring came the Easter holiday and Easter eggs. The Sunday before Easter was 'Palm Sunday' when, for obscure reasons, to symbolise the palm leaves in the Bible stories, we had to have a bunch of pussy willow in the house. Just a vase of it, but it had to have the fluffy pussy willow catkins on or it wasn't proper 'palm'. It was my job to get it. This was easy because there were only a couple of pussy willow trees and they were close together.

Mum had been brought up a strict, even fundamentalist, Anglican. Her father was a devout man who read the Bible every evening – when we had to be absolutely quiet – even using a magnifying glass to see the small print in his Bible. It was the Bible he had carried with him as a shepherd and which he read every day in his hut while minding his sheep. It might well have been the only book he had ever read. He said it was the only book we needed – which was daft because it didn't have anything about bird's eggs or different types of fish in it or what was the best bait to use.

Our grandfather died when I was three years old but I still remember how we were not allowed to play or whistle or even laugh on Sunday and the only things we could look at was a Bible or a prayer book, never a comic or a children's picture book. Sundays were not happy days; they were boring, solemn days when we wore our Sunday best, put this week's clean underwear on, and couldn't go out to play.

Being able to read and write was a skill in my grandfather's generation which many did not possess, so he was generally admired. Shepherds were considered a cut above the ordinary farm labourers. They were the aristocrats of the farm labouring classes. They had a special skill to sell and my grandfather was one of the best. He had the rosettes and medals to prove it, won in the agricultural shows he used to show his sheep at. He ended up at Fawler because he had been head–hunted by a farmer with a prize flock.

To begin with, my parents sent us to Sunday School at Finstock Church but later, after her father died, and because of the distance it meant walking, these became infrequent then stopped altogether. My father, whose family had been Primitive Methodists, steeped in the temperance movement that had inspired their puritanical Wesleyan breakaway movement from mainstream Methodism, was not especially religious but he viewed alcohol with more than a little suspicion. He was born 'out of wedlock' and his mother never had him baptised because she didn't want "them hypocrites to get their 'ands on 'im".

He had spent three years in India during the war and spoke Hindi. He once said, 'when you see those people in India with their own religions, how do you know they're wrong and we're right?' Mum told him not to be so daft, but it was a thought that stuck with me for a very long time and was to have a profound effect on me later.

Easter was a confused sort of holiday. It wasn't obvious where eggs and chocolate came into it but it had something to do with Jesus being crucified and coming back to life again, and palm leaves and people shouting 'hosanna!' It all seemed rather odd to me. Were we still supposed to hate the Jews for killing Jesus even after what had happened during the war? People still said that what Hitler had done to them was just what they deserved but others were now saying it was a terrible crime and that we should be friends with the Jews because they had suffered enough and deserved their own country again.

But what difference had killing Jesus made anyway if he just came back to life afterwards? How did this 'save' me and help God forgive me? And why had the Jews been wicked if God had wanted Jesus to be killed? It just didn't make sense, but the chocolate eggs were good.

So, after 'Good Friday' – 'good' because the wicked Jews had killed Jesus according to God's plan, apparently! – then it was Easter Sunday with the eggs, then Easter Monday which seemed just like another Sunday. Had Jesus gone to heaven while still alive on Easter Monday? No-one seemed very sure on that point but he had definitely come back to life – as a holy ghost!

Anyway, with Easter out of the way, summer emerged from spring quietly and unannounced. The days got longer and warmer and we had time to go out to play after tea before it got dark. We even went to bed in daylight!

School was over for the six whole weeks that seemed like a lifetime, we swam and fished in the Evenlode, climbed trees in the woods, punted our rafts, hunted adders along the hedgerows and, come September, looked for delicious fresh mushrooms in the water meadows. We generally found something to do every day, even if it was to gather together in one of the disused pigsties in the rain and plan our next expedition.

But with just a few of us, it only needed one to not be coming out today and another to be out for the day, maybe in Oxford or Witney, and I was alone. On these days, feeling lonely and friendless, I would wander along the river bank or maybe sit and fish, or just stroll along the lane towards Northleigh looking at nature and trying to make sense of it all. Why were oak leaves that shape and different to elm leaves? Why did different trees have different bark? Why were there different butterflies and different wild flowers? Was it really all there just for humans?

What did a peacock butterfly or a wild dog-rose do for humans other than look pretty and what difference would it make to us if they weren't there? Yet we were told God had made them just for us. Why then were there 'vermin' that the game keepers needed to kill?

It seemed obvious to me even at an early age that this couldn't all be for us humans and that there must be another reason why there were so many different animals, birds, insects and plants, most of which we couldn't eat and some of which were poisonous. What was this all for, exactly?

At the end of summer, when the corn was ripe and ready, the farm went into harvest mode. Work began early in the morning and last until dark. It would take a day to cut a field with a combined harvester and a constant stream of tractors went out to the field to get a cart–load of corn and bring it back to the farmyard for sifting and bagging.

The cart was tipped up and the corn shot into a makeshift pen surrounded by corrugated iron sheets. From here it was picked up in oval cups mounted on a continuous belt and taken to the top of the sifter. From there it descended though a series of moving sieves to separate the chaff and the weed seeds – mostly poppy – to leave a more–or–less clean stream of wheat, barley or oats to pass down a chute into a hessian sack. As this was filled, the chute was closed off as the bag was tied and another put in its place. The bags were then taken off to be manhandled into a storage loft in the adjacent building.

The sifter was powered by an ancient tractor via a continuous belt and it was the sound of this tractor which alerted the children to the need for child labour – and to the prospect of a ride in the corn carts.

The one mechanical problem that the set–up had not solved was how to keep the corn in the pen moving into the cups on the conveyor belt. This required lots of children armed with long–handled shovels, some with handles taller than we were. Our reward was a ride in the cart out to the field, to stand under the stream of corn as it came out of the combined harvester, and a ride back to the farmyard. Occasionally, we would stay with the 'combine', especially when it was getting close to the last few square yards of standing corn – where the hares and pheasants had gradually been driven. The driver had a loaded 12–bore, double–barrelled shotgun. Our job was to go and fetch the hare or pheasant.

Later, the sifter was replaced with a newer machine which also dried the corn and the corn was shot into a tapered silo. The corn was picked up by a rotating Archimedean screw. It would have been dangerous to allow us children anywhere near it. I often wonder who would have done this essential job if we children had not been around and willing. Maybe the children had always worked on the farms, helping out when needed. The family worked for the farmer, not just the husband.

With the harvest in and summer nearly over it was time to begin building the bonfire again and another year had come and gone in a hamlet that had seen little change over the centuries. We were vaguely aware that things were changing and had begun to change after the war, but we had no idea how or why. But we knew the age of deference was almost over.

In The Blink Of An Eye

6. Myxy Sticks and Mercy Killing

Baby rabbits with eyes full of puss,
This is the work of scientific us!

Spike Milligan

In the Coronation year of 1953 something happened that was to have a profound effect on the English countryside; the rabbit disease, myxomatosis, was introduced in an attempt to control the rabbit population.

The rabbit, although familiar to everyone and certainly now an integral part of the British countryside, is not a native species. It is believed to have been introduced from Iberia by the Romans. It was semi domesticated, being kept for food in specially constructed warrens. A warren, managed by a warrener, is a walled enclosure surrounding a sandy bank in which the rabbits made their burrow. It did not seem to survive to form breeding feral populations until the Early Middle Ages, when maybe a genetic or environmental change made it possible.

During the first onslaught of rabbit myxomatosis the countryside suddenly became full of pathetic 'myxy' rabbits. They staggered blindly (and deafly) about, their eyes and ears swollen and closed with hideous pustules, completely lost and disorientated. They were squashed by cars, killed by dogs, cats and foxes, and were dispatched mercifully by us humans who carried our 'myxy sticks' with a notch cut in the shaft for every rabbit dispatched.

They wandered into village streets and gardens completely oblivious of their surroundings, relying solely on blundering into something edible by chance.

The foxes had a brief heyday and their population exploded for a year or so, then, almost as quickly as it had hit the rabbit population like some plague of biblical proportions, it was over. The rabbits had gone. Where once you could watch twenty or thirty rabbits run for their burrows as you popped your head over a wall or held your baby brother or sister up to see them, they were no more. In their place the countryside was littered with beached white skeletons under hedges and bushes where once there had been burrows and bunnies galore. You could pick up half a dozen rabbit skulls on a short country walk.

People predicted the complete extinction of the rabbit and hotly debated what right farmers had to exterminate an animal that had once been a major free food item for country folk. A good rabbit stew, with carrots, swedes, onions and potatoes, and maybe a few chopped up cabbage leaves or turnip tops, could feed a small family for several days. Now the sight of 'myxy' put many people off rabbit and a free meal that had served country folk well since the Middle Ages and with which they had so recently eked out the meagre war–time rations, dropped off the menu.

I once killed twenty rabbits in the corner of a single field in a few minutes. You had to be careful how you handled a myxy stick as the wrong end was a gory, pussy mess. You could easily spot a distant myxy rabbit because the swelling exposed the pale under-fur making it look like they had pale bases to their ears and pale stripes over their eyes.

Myxy Sticks and Mercy Killing

ooOoo

At the bottom of the Nuttery you climbed through the fence and into a field. There were always a lot of rabbits in this field but sadly, just after the war, myxomatosis was introduced to keep the rabbit population down. This was a dreadful disease; the poor rabbits died a slow and lingering death. We felt it our duty to go and put these poor creatures out of their misery, so with a stout stick we went "Rabbiting". They were easy to catch as most of them were blind. We used to creep up to them and grab them by the ears and with one swift blow strike them on the back of their head. They died instantly. Then using our pen knives we cut notches into our sticks to keep a count of how many we killed.

I can't believe I used to do this, but we thought we were doing the Rabbits a favour.

ooOoo

It looked for a while as though the ubiquitous rabbit, the farmer's enemy and the friend to every villager who had a family to feed and who knew how to set a snare or work a ferret, was about to disappear forever.

With a good ferret, if you knew where the best burrows were, you could get enough rabbits in an hour to feed a family for a week. By next year the burrow would be full of rabbits again as each female could rear a batch of half a dozen young every three months and the young would be breeding themselves almost before the next batch had left the nest. You had to know which burrows were ready for the next rabbit harvest.

And then there were reports of a few rabbits being seen again. Had they become resistant? There were stories of a change of habit with rabbits abandoning the burrowing life and living above ground like hares. I

93

didn't believe a word of it. Hares give birth to a fully–developed leveret, able to run and even feed itself in a matter of minutes; rabbits are born blind and helpless and barely able to walk for three weeks. They would never survive above ground.

And it was not to last. The rabbit population began to recover, as it can do very quickly given the high birth rate and rapid maturity. Then another wave of myxy struck.

But gradually, over the years, the populations recovered more quickly and each wave of myxy killed fewer. Nowadays, myxy rabbits are unusual and the population is back to its pre–1950s level. I haven't seen a myxy rabbit for about five years.

The rabbit evolved resistance and the myxoma virus attenuated. After the first few waves the rabbit population was too small for the virus to infect new victims before it killed its host. With a low rabbit population the virus itself was threatened with extinction, so natural selection favoured those which didn't always kill their victims but allowed them to live at least long enough to infect other rabbits.

Natural selection favoured those rabbits which didn't die. Just as humans and the Black Death organism (almost certainly the *Yersina pestis* bacterium) reached an accommodation, so rabbits and myxoma 'learned' to live with one another.

To me, this seemed such an obvious explanation that I couldn't understand why people ever doubted it. I don't remember reading this explanation anywhere and, at that stage in my life I knew nothing of formal evolutionary theory or genetics – but what else could possibly have caused this change and stopped myxy killing off the rabbits still?

Nature seems a rather wonderful, if savage and merciless thing. The rabbits that myxy had killed had actually benefitted future rabbits because they left the field (literally) clear for resistant rabbits and the rabbit species was the winner. Nature is not sentimental but nature works.

So, we saw in the failed myxomatosis experiment that nature has a few tricks up her metaphorical sleeve and can sometime bounce back into a dynamic balance quite quickly. It is not always so, however.

We may have lost for good a couple of our once–familiar vertebrates: the red squirrel and the water vole. It looked for a time that the otter may be on the way out too but there are promising signs of a sustained recovery.

The red squirrel and the water vole are both victims of human interference, the latter a victim of the ignorantly stupid but well– intentioned animal right activists who let mink out of their cages in protest at the inhumane conditioned they were kept in in fur farms. The mink is an aggressive North American predatory species which will eat just about anything it can catch and is well–adapted for a semi–aquatic life. It set about predating on the humble water vole and has just about exterminated it over much of its range.

The once common, even abundant, water vole now teeters on the brink of extinction, sustained for the most part only by carefully managed breeding and release programs coupled with mink trapping and extermination programs. If you're walking along an Oxfordshire river nowadays and think you've seen a dark brown otter, you've almost certainly seen a mink. It has a pointed nose; not the rounded snout of the otter.

The beautiful red squirrel is, to all intents and purposes, extinct in much of the British mainland, though it continued to thrive in off–shore islands and in a few refuges in the Scottish Highlands.

When once they were common in the woods around Fawler, I saw my last red squirrel probably in about 1958, maybe as late as 1960. For a while it had been a bit of a game to identify if it was a red or a grey as a squirrel scampered through the branches above us.

I was fishing quietly when I heard a frequent plopping sound of something being dropped into the river about 20 yards away and on the other bank. I listened quietly and there is was again! It didn't sound like a fish rising but what could be making things fall from the over–hanging tree?

Slowly I walked along the bank in best stealth mode until I saw a red squirrel in an over–hanging hazel nut tree, picking under–ripe nuts, biting the shells open and eating the nut, then dropping the shells into the river. I watched it transfixed for about five minutes – then it saw me and was gone. It was the last wild red squirrel I ever saw until I saw some in France many years later.

The red squirrel has been the victim of the introduced North American cousin species, the grey squirrel. The reasons for the grey's success is partly to do with its more robust build and more aggressive nature in that it can easily drive the red out of the niche they both need to occupy to survive. But it is probably mostly due to germ warfare. The grey carries the parapox virus which is fatal to reds but harmless to greys.

The greys have failed to displace the reds in parts of Europe where squirrel parapox is not endemic.

Recently, it has been noticed that, in Ireland, where the pine marten has been reintroduced, this has led to a surprising increase in the population of red squirrels. The reason is believed to be due to the pine marten predating more on greys than the more agile red, so allowing the reds to bounce back. It might be that the introduction of greys had such a devastating effect on reds in Britain because it coincided with the decline due to persecution of the pine marten.

The reason greys are less successful against the pine marten is probably because, in North America, where they evolved, their range does not overlap that of the North American martens. The European reds however evolved in the presence of pine martens so they evolved greater agility or some other escape method that the greys lack.

7. School Days

The cloakroom pegs are empty now,
And locked the classroom door,
The hollow desks are lined with dust,
And slow across the floor
A sunbeam creeps between the chairs
Till the sun shines no more.

Philip Larkin

Fawler children went to primary school at Finstock – the little Church of England school where three teachers taught us to read, write and do arithmetic, and even managed to fit in a little geography, history and music. Very occasionally one or two children would pass the 11 plus and go to Chipping Norton Grammar School; the rest of us went to Spendlove Secondary School in nearby Charlbury. It seemed strange how often the only children to pass the 11 plus had only come to the school in the final year or two, while those of us who had spent all out school years there normally failed.

To get to Finstock School, Fawler children were lucky. Although we lived less than the statutory two miles away, so did not qualify for a school bus, the bus which picked up the Chipping Norton Grammar School children came through Fawler, picked up the few Grammar School children there, and picked up the next group at the end of School Road, Finstock. So, we got a free lift, only needing to walk the couple of hundred yards to school.

Returning home was a different matter as the Grammar School bus came along too late. We walked home the mile and half to Fawler in all weathers, the older children taking responsibility for the younger ones. We did that journey four days a week, the exception being Thursday.

Thursday was market day in Witney so the local bus company, Worth's Buses of Enstone, put on a coach to Witney in the morning and back in the afternoon. It came through Finstock about ten minutes before school normally finished. To save money and to get a free lift to market, Wally Scarrott acted as bus conductor and, because his daughters went to Finstock School, part of the deal was that the school children got a free lift. All we had to do was leave school early and hurry along to the end of School Road to catch the bus. Part of the deal too was that we helped Wally carry his boxes of supplied down to his shop.

ooOoo

We caught Worth's bus in the morning it was the Chipping Norton Grammar School bus. It came through Fawler from Stonesfield but it used to pick us up and drop us off at the bottom of School Road. It then turned round and went on to Charlbury and all the other villages en route to Chipping Norton.

At night we had to walk home. It was just less than two miles. The older kids looked after the younger ones. Of course there was hardly any traffic in those days and what there was went so slowly we had time to keep to the side to let it pass.

We used to have such fun on the way home. Looking for birds nest in the hedgerows and keeping an eye on it, waiting for the eggs to hatch so we could see the baby chicks and when they had flown we could take the nest to school to show the rest of the class.

Going down Finstock Hill we had to go over three bridges. The first was the railway bridge. If we timed it right, we could hear a train coming from Charlbury. We would run like mad and hang over the bridge and with stone in hand, wait for it to come under the bridge. As it came out the other side we tried to drop the stone down the funnel of course we never knew whether we were on target or not because we used to get covered in smoke, but it seemed like a good idea at the time.

The next bridge was over the river. This time we had races with sticks or leaves floating through.

The third bridge was over the mill stream. On the left of the road stands an old mill house; the wheel long gone even then. I can remember an Italian family called Dettoro living there. They later moved to oxford. There were always kingfishers in the mill stream. We used to stand for ages watching them.

ooOoo

The school day would start with morning assembly where we all gathered together in the main classroom, sang a hymn and said prayers with our hands together and our eyes closed.

Probably the one saving grace for me in the morning assembly was that we would occasionally sing a hymn that had the words "will obey" in it. I could shut my eyes and picture this Willow Bay, with its sky–blue sea gently lapping on golden sands and fringed with weeping willow trees. Wherever in the world Willow Bay was, probably on a tropical island, I determined to go there one day. Hopefully, there would not be cannibals.

But that was one little ray of sunshine in an otherwise long, drawn out hour of tedium and terror. Was it an hour? It seemed like two but it was probably little more than twenty minutes.

I remember watching a Denis Potter play on TV some years ago in which children were standing in class to say the Lord's Prayer, when, on the words, "forgive us our trespasses", the teacher stepped forward and hit a boy hard across the face for opening his eyes. It was eerily reminiscent! It could have been Finstock C of E Primary School in 1955.

I witnessed an identical incident and still remember feeling that sudden burn of indignation at the injustice and hypocrisy of it. She must have had her eyes open! And she was not forgiving anyone! Was this why I started to question religion? The devout always seemed so very un–Christian!

Primary school was not a happy time for me. It was not the work that bothered me – I was actually quite a clever boy who could read well and do 'sums' without too much difficulty. I was probably not the cleverest but I learned my 'tables' easily and rose to my 'level of expectation', which, from the teachers' perspective, was low because my parents were 'lowly' people and little was expected of us. The 'posh' children were fawned over by the teachers, especially the headmistress, Miss Hope, who was an inveterate snob.

She seemed to get some sort of sadistic pleasure from caning boys across outstretched bare hands – one hand for the less serious 'crime' like having a fountain pen that dropped blobs of ink, and both hands for the more serious crimes like answering back or being left–handed. She caned one boy unmercifully because he went to the book cupboard and got a book on British birds to show her that there really was a bird called a great tit! She had crossed out 'great' and had written 'small' in red ink over it.

The crime was having answered her back! The real crime was being right when she was wrong! It was a crime to be right when the teacher was wrong! I knew there were great tits; how come she didn't? Teachers were supposed to know everything, weren't they? At least we thought so. Why else were they teachers if they didn't know everything? We went to school to learn everything so surely the teachers should know everything, shouldn't they?

And some poor kid was being made to suffer for her incompetence and inability to admit a mistake! She was wrong, and I knew she was wrong! And she said prayers, talked to us about God and Jesus and played the church organ on Sundays! And punished children for showing her she was wrong!

It seemed to me that barely a day went by without at least one boy being caned in front of the whole class. She would cane left–handed children for holding their knife and fork in the 'wrong' hands or for writing with their left hand. Left–handedness was a sin to be beaten out of them. They used their left hand not because it was natural for them to do so but to show defiance and disobedience. In her eyes they literally were sinister.

The biblical slogan, "spare the rod and spoil the child", was almost the school motto. I was caned four times. On one occasion I could barely hold my knife and fork to eat my school dinner. We sat two to a desk and shared most textbook. My crime had been to not be able to find a book – which was in my partner's drawer – and keeping the class waiting. After dinner, with still painful fingers, we had to write 'I must not keep the class waiting' 100 times instead of being able to play in the playground.

The head mistress was a friend of the local vicar and played the church organ on Sundays. She lived with two other ladies in the school house. Our parent's view was, typically of the deferential society they had been brought up in, that we must have done something to deserve it. A teacher wouldn't cane us for nothing.

There were two other teachers: a female teacher who taught the juniors in their first two years and a male teacher who taught us for the next two years. We then spent the final two or three years with the head mistress.

The junior's teacher had grey hair turned yellow at the front by the cigarettes she chain smoked in the class room. She literally lit her next cigarette with her previous one. If she ran out of cigarettes two of us would be dispatched to Mrs Dore's shop along the road to buy her 20 Craven A. We might even be given a penny for doing it. If it was Thursday, when the shop was closed in the afternoon, we had to run down to the Plough Inn about half a mile away, and 'come straight back'.

Her favourite punishment was to rap our knuckles with a wooden ruler, edge on for a serious crime. I was only 'rulered' once for whistling when she told us how Jesus had filled enough baskets with bread and fish to feed 5000 people from just the crumbs left over from a few loaves and fishes! Maybe she thought I was expressing some doubt!

"Please Miss! Why didn't Jesus just fill the baskets with the loaves and fishes? Why did the disciples have to make the crumbs first"? No, I never asked the question but I thought it afterwards. You didn't risk a caning by questioning what Jesus did! It was Gospel! It was real history and was written down by someone who was there!

Maybe it was the shock of the rulering that made the story stick in my mind.

The male teacher, who must remain anonymous, was actually a very good teacher and illustrated his lessons with drawings he had done himself. He taught us the rudiments of history with drawings of cave men, Greek heroes, Roman soldiers, Egyptian Pharos and Spanish Armadas.

He would call us to his desk to stand by his side as he went through our 'composition' about what we did at the week end, or to show us why this or that sum was wrong and how to get the right answer. All the while, hidden by his desk, he would lovingly put his hand round our thighs and pull us closer to him. Then he would slip his hand up the leg of our short trousers and carefully check that everything was as it should be down there. He was such a nice man. So far as I know, only boys got this special care. If girls did, they never said anything. It never felt like abuse at the time.

Sadly, or maybe not so sadly because the uproar might have left us even more traumatized, this was not something we could tell our parents (I assume others felt pretty much the way I did) because we would probably have got a wallop for "Coming out with something like that! Whatever will he come out with next?" You see, even knowing it was wrong to be touched by a man would have given away that we knew about such things! Anyway, I don't think any of us really realised it was wrong. It was just what he did and it didn't hurt, or anything.

So deference, the taboo against talking about our 'private parts' and the fear of parental disapproval, all conspired to keep this sort of thing out of the public domain and to allow the abusers to abuse, almost immune from sanction and safe in the reliable conspiracy of silence.

ooOoo

Miss Hope was the head mistress of the school. Mrs Busby taught the infants and Mr Warner the middle class. Later, Mr Picken came and replaced Mr Warner. Miss Hope lived in the school house with Miss Packer and Miss Powell. Miss Packer had been the former head mistress; Miss Powell was the house keeper.

From the day I started school I had to sit at a desk and sit still; discipline was very strict. I learnt to write using a slate and chalk. I sat next to Margaret Townsend. She was one of a large family who lived up Church Rise.

I can remember once being accused of ruffling up some papers.. Mrs Bushy did not believe me when I said I didn't do it. I was made to stand out in front of the class and was given the 'ruler' across the hand. I must have been about seven at the time. I can also remember being naughty and being shut in a large store–cupboard and forgotten. If my brother had not looked for me after school, I would have still been there next morning.

In the morning everyone went in to Miss Hope's classroom for assembly. Everyone stood, either at their desks or in a straight line at the side of the room. Prayers were said and hymns were sung.

It was also time for any punishment to be given. If any of the boys had done something wrong then they were given the cane in front of the school. Even if you had been naughty outside school hours Miss hope always knew. I can remember crying my eyes out when Bill was caned once. I don't know what it was for but we dare not tell Mum or Dad when we got home or we would get another good hiding, usually from Mum.

ooOoo

The feature of the school year was the Christmas concert. Rehearsals started straight away after the summer holidays. Parts were allocated in the plays; members of the dance teams and choirs were chosen and lines written out to be memorised.

Rehearsals seemed endless, several times a week as the big day approached and at least one full 'dress' rehearsal at the village hall. Costumes were made and adjusted to fit; we must have used miles of crepe paper and cardboard and gallons of gold and silver paint.

For some reason, I only ever had small parts in the plays with a couple of lines to learn. The best parts obviously went to the children with the more important parents and I didn't qualify.

But I could sing reasonably well, even in tune. I could actually sing the scales! So, I sang the solo male part in "On Yonder Hill" and got a really loud clap! I was picked to sing in the school choir which sang at the Oxford Music Festival in the Sheldonian Theatre! How we sniggered at the naked cherubs painted on the ceiling beneath Sir Christopher Wren's dome.

Music was taught to us via the radio! We had got a radio in the school in about 1952. I remember the death of the King being announced on it. There were three schools programs in particular that all had a profound influence on me.

The first was a music program which was accompanied by a booklet with music in it. By simply going through the music a step at a time, first tapping out the rhythm while following the notes, then la–la–laing the tune, we learned to read music. I even understood about treble and bass clefs, sharps and flats, minims, crotchets and quavers and soon could sing from the music. It felt good to be able to read music like a code! I could read a knitting pattern too, but that's another story! Yes, Mum taught me to knit along with my sisters, though I never knitted my own cardigans like they did!

It never seemed significant to me that I liked repetitive patterns and logical stuff like music and knitting patterns and learning about birds and animals and cataloguing information in my mind! Learning stuff was just fun and felt good! What did we know about the Asperger's spectrum? I was just clever and liked learning things! Anyway, I was only border–line and only slightly socially handicapped by it. Later in life when I learned to write computer code I found I could relax and lose myself in coding.

Some of the songs we learned were English, Welsh and Scottish folk songs, 'Collected by Ralph Vaughan Williams' (what a funny name to read!) When your name is William it's something special to see someone with it as a surname, but 'Rayf'? How was that 'Rayf'? And 'Vawn'! So, Ralf Vowghan Williams collected folk songs!

And so did 'Cecil Sharpe'. Wonderful songs like, 'Twas on a Monday Morning, O' and 'On Yonder Hill'. Yonder! 'Twas! 'Ne'er!', 'Beheld!' Wonderful words, full of olden times and days of yore! Tunes you could sing and rhythms to tap your foot to! Sea shanties – 'Way, haul away! We'll haul away the bo'line! Way haul away! Haul away Joe!' – and Fife and Drum tunes. Maidens and Green Grow the Rushes O! (was that about my beautiful Evenlode where the rushes grew a green o!).

Imagine if you will the delights of learning to sing:

> O soldier, soldier, won't you marry me
> With your musket, fife and drum?
> O no sweet maid I cannot marry you
> For I have no coat to put on.
> So up she went to her grandfather's chest
> And she got him a coat of the very, very best
> And the soldier put it on.

With its rhythm, its repetition, its misogynistic humour, what more could an impressionable, border–line Asperger's boy with four sisters and an ear for music want in a song?!

One proud day, I was the only child in the class who could read the name Tchaikovsky!

The second radio program was about nature! Oh the joy of a radio program about nature! All about birds, badgers and beetles; cockchafers, cuckoos and cadis flies, and things starting with other letters of the alphabet! Even stuff I already knew because I had read it in my nature books! It was all set in somewhere called Cowleas Farm. Was this in Cowley, Oxford? I thought it probably was.

And then the teacher spoiled it by making us draw a picture about what we had just heard! It wasn't about drawing! It was about nature! I could write down the life–cycle of a peacock butterfly or describe the metamorphosis of a tadpole into a frog, but I couldn't draw one!

The third program, and the one which was to have a profound effect on me in a way that was probably not intended by the producers or the government which sponsored it, was History!

For some reason which I have never understood, 'history' included Greek and Roman mythology. Maybe the production team thought it really **was** history and who were we to argue. History was about things that had really happened a long time ago before anyone alive today could remember. We were being taught a history in which magic was real! There were monsters with one eye. There were heroes whose mother had dipped them in the River Styx to protect them because a god told her to!

There were giants on mountains holding up the sky and their daughters could still be seen in the sky as the Pleiades cluster if you looked carefully in the right place, and there was Orion hunting them with his dog Sirius!

There were Gorgons with snakes for hair. They could turn you to stone with a look, and there were lots of gods who people spoke to and who spoke back and who could make impossible things happen like dragon's teeth turning into warriors! These were gods who people believed in and who actually spoke and made themselves visible.

And this was real history! This really happened, or we thought it did!

How could this be so? Didn't we now know without a shadow of a doubt that there is and always has been only one god, and he only ever spoke to Jews in Hebrews, Latin or old–fashioned English? We knew this because it was in the Bible and the Bible was God's Holy Word. There could be no doubt about this at all! It was wrong to even question the Bible!

The Greeks and Romans; the Persians and Egyptians; the Ancient Norse and the 'Pagans' must have been mistaken. And yet they heard these gods and these gods made magic happen and helped Jason find the Golden Fleece and turned themselves into white bulls or swans and had children! Apollo and Zeus; Aphrodite and Horus; Diana and Atlas; these had all been real once upon a time, hadn't they?

Well, that was just silly because the Jews had been told the truth by the one true God. Their history was the real history. There is only one god and He had caused a flood and led the Hebrew slaves out of Egypt with its false gods. False gods! False gods that they spoke to! How did they get it so wrong? All of them! Everyone apart from the Hebrews got everything wrong!

Then, to cap it all, when the Romans ran Judea, the Jews suddenly got everything wrong too! For some reason, although they had been word–perfect about everything else, when it came to Jesus, and mankind was about to be saved, the Jews went off message and got it all wrong too!

Now the Romans suddenly got it all right and have done so ever since. Well, nearly because they are still Catholics and haven't realised yet that the Church of England is the One True Faith, but at least they believe in Jesus and the One True God.

But why did the Greeks and Romans and all those people who had different gods in their history get it so wrong and even chatted to their gods and saw their gods doing magic things!

It didn't make sense! It worried me. This was history – the stuff that really happened – and it couldn't have happened! But why were they wrong and only the Hebrews right? Why were the Hebrew stories truth and all the others made up?

At the end of term, as good Christian children attending a Church of England school, we went to an end–of–term church service. I was nine and was sitting in church looking around and feeling very holy and pious when I saw God. He was in a stained–glass window and dressed in a purple Roman toga! It might not have been God, but it was someone holy and he wore a Roman toga! But I thought it was God.

I remember to this day the physical feeling of a light switching on in my mind. I was having an irreligious experience!

God was a Roman myth! Christianity was a Roman myth, just like all the other myths from 'history'! The question which had been worrying me suddenly had a spectacular and totally unexpected answer. I never went into church seeking answers or particularly troubled but I came out with one anyway and one that forced itself on me without my permission.

How could they have got it wrong so only one 'history' was the right one? Why had the Jews suddenly got it wrong and now the Romans were right, having been wrong before?

They couldn't all be right, and there was no reason why only one should be. They couldn't all be right, **but they could all be wrong!**

They **were** all wrong! The God of the Hebrews; the God of the Bible; the Holy Word of God! They were all myths! The Bible was a book of myths. Interesting, exciting in parts; scary in others, even beautiful literature in places, but it was a story. It was a myth.

Man created god in his own image!

I came out of church a changed person. I came out into a bright, exciting world full of light and things than were shouting out to be understood! Oh, there were mysteries alright, but they were mysteries which **could** be understood, eventually. I stepped out of church into a rational world that I wanted to understand! I wanted what I later learned was science!

I have been an atheist ever since.

I appreciate that not everyone sees things this way. If you are offended then I would ask you to consider the following:

There has been something in the order of 2,500–3,000 gods people have believed in. Believers will find it hard to believe, but they are only one god different to me. Would you think anyone should be offended because you don't believe in Zeus or Wotan, Ra or Aphrodite? We agree about almost all gods – and for exactly the same reason I don't believe in yours, if you have one.

So, the schools radio service which taught us mythology as history taught me something that was probably farthest from the mind of the producers at the time.

Anyway, back to my childhood and school days.

Once a year we had the dreadful news that the school dentist would be visiting next week! We took a note home so our parents could give their permission for us to be seen by him. He was a huge monster of a man who so it was rumoured by those not needing treatment, hated children. He had red hair and hairy arms like a bear!

A few days later we got the even more dreadful news that we needed some dental work. The worst of all possible news would be that we needed an extraction!

On the dreaded day, normal lessons would be suspended as one class room was turned into what can only be described as a torture chamber. Those needing treatment would sit outside, listening to the screams and sobs next door, waiting for our name to be called. We were shown into the presence of the child–hating, hairy brute and he smiled at us! He was enjoying it!

Around the wall sat the children with whom he had finished; their cheeks swollen with the blood–soaked cotton wool, dribbling blood–stained saliva out of the corner of a paralysed mouth and sobbing in pain. They were trying to look interested in an old copy of Beano or Dandy that had been thrust into their hands by his female accomplice! It was how I imagined a field hospital in the Crimea would have looked!

Then we climbed into the chair which was suddenly tilted back. The accomplice grabbed our head. "Open wide!" And a hypodermic needle was whipped out from behind the monster's back, an onion–flavoured finger was put into our mouth and the needle was jabbed painfully into the roof of our mouth and our gums. A searing pain shot up the side of our face and a bitter taste of cocaine spread across our mouth. Then our head was held in a vice–like grip, a pair of pliers was thrust into our mouth and the inside of our face was pulled out! We tried not to scream!

And a bloody tooth was dropped with a clang into a metal dish. A wad of cotton wool was stuffed into the bleeding wound; we were told to bite hard, and then we realised we couldn't feel ourselves biting. The whole side of our face was beginning to go numb. We tried to talk but only one side of our mouth worked. Then we had to sit for a while and read the Beano or Dandy, and tried not to dribble.

It was years before I could pluck up the courage to go to a dentist. It was not until, aged about twenty–one, a painful maxillary abscess had kept me awake for a couple of nights that I decided maybe another session in the torture chamber was slightly less daunting than trying to pull the infected tooth out myself.

In the days before water fluoridisation and fluoridated tooth–paste, hollow teeth and gumboils were common. Oil of cloves rubbed unto the gum gave some relief and left your gum and the side of your tongue numb for an hour or two. I quite liked the taste too. The idea of free dental care on the NHS seemed not to have entered the consciousness of our parents' generation and anyway it would have meant a day trip to Witney or Chipping Norton, or maybe Woodstock or Oxford.

A few years after I left Finstock School, following an enquiry into the very low 11–Plus pass–rate after there had been no passes for four years, the school was ordered to stop wasting time on the Christmas concerts. So bad had been the academic standards that, when we went to the secondary school, they had been concerned at our low level of achievement in the streaming tests we took. Along with all my classmates from Finstock School in 1958, we were 'B' streamed. At the end of the first year, three of us had been restreamed as 'A' stream, two of us from Fawler, myself and my beautiful country dance partner.

I was 'clever', but had been 'B' streamed. By the end of the first year I was helping out the teachers by taking a remedial reading group! I came top of the year in Science and Geography (the end of term exams had been identical for all streams). I won the Geography Prize (a book on British birds) and was denied the Science Prize because we could only win one prize per person.

On the last science lesson of that year I took the class for science because I had scored almost 100% in the end of term exam so the science teacher asked me to go through the exam paper with the class while he marked some other papers. I actually found it strangely exhilarating! Suddenly, I was "Good at Science"! And I was best at something other than athletics.

By any normal standards I and several other Finstock School children should have gone to Grammar School and should have been given a chance to go to university. I left school in 1963 with four GCE 'O' levels and it took me until 1971 to get two more 'O' levels, an Ordinary National Certificate in Science and a Higher National Certificate (a BA equivalent) in Applied Biology. For some reason, I struggled with 'O' level English, sitting it five times before getting a minimal pass grade. I have never been able to make sense of the vageries of English speling, being border–line Asperger's and preferring sensible rools! However did people manage without spell–checkers?

I was an athlete!

I used to win races because I was tall for my age and had good, strong National Health legs fed on National Health orange juice, cod liver oil, free school milk and cheap school dinners. And I was okay at football. I could kick the ball a long way and could run fast, so I was a good full–back or winger. I was even in the school team for a while – until my love of nature put an end to that!

Football was not a game for sissies. The leather ball absorbed about ten pounds of water no matter how much 'dubbing' had been rubbed into it and it had a lethal lace that would lacerate the head of anyone foolish enough to head it. Football boots were real leather boots that came up over the ankle to protect it from the wooden block of a toecap. Studs were made of hardened leather discs through which four nails were driven into the wooden sole. As the leather wore down the nails drove further into and then through the sole – and into the foot.

As your foot grew your big toe pushed up against the wooden toecap so that when you kicked the ball, which by now probably weighed about 28 pounds, the wooden toecap broke the nail on your big toe. In those days, a football boot with its wooden toecap and nail–headed leather studs was a lethal weapon and your leg was lucky to come out of a tackle with its skin intact.

By the end of the game, especially if you didn't have shin pads, your shins would be bruised and bleeding, and your boot would be full of blood. Prising off the boots, which were now nailed to your feet, was a painful process, as was walking afterwards. And I'm really not exaggerating – very much.

This was carried out once a week in all weathers in winter, in mud, snow and ice and the school had no showers. It was good for the character, apparently!

Then one day my promising football career came to an abrupt end.

We were playing in a six–a–side tournament at Minster Lovell and I was positioned in defence. In a six–a–side competition, in the event of a draw, corners count.

It was a beautiful, cloud–free day and the play was up the other end of the field when I saw a kestrel hovering nearby! I stood transfixed watching, waiting for the dive and hoping to see if it had made a kill as it flew up again, my heart pounding with excitement.

Suddenly the play came streaming past me and I heard someone screaming my name from the side–line. And the kestrel was still hovering…

What could I do? This was important!

So, thinking quickly, I sprinted back, overtook the play and lofted the ball for a corner! Phew! Now, where was that kestrel? It had gone!

And we lost by that single corner and were out of the tournament in the first round! For some reason everyone blamed me! But it was a kestrel, and it was hovering!

The next morning the entire school was informed in assembly that we had lost because of me and I would never play for the school again. I never did.

My cricket career was even less successful. I had two batting strokes – a slog and a slog which missed the ball. For some unfathomable reason we were expected to stand there while someone threw a really hard ball at you and your only defence against a split lip, a broken nose or a fractured skull was to hit it with a bat before it hit you, and to try not to break your fingers by getting the timing slightly wrong.

Then, if you managed to hit it, someone came running down the pitch shouting "Run!" at you, and you had to run in the other direction while someone again threw the hard ball at you! And just because you ran into the stumps or were too slow, or you collided with the person running in the other direction and you both fell over, you had to go and sit on the side while they did it to someone else.

And people did this for fun on Sundays!

I vaguely remember playing for the school once, but I could be wrong. Maybe there were a lot off sick that day.

But I was an athlete and used to win races! I was going to run in the Olympics and break the four minute mile, like Roger Banister had! I was also good at jumping. I could high jump higher and long jump longer than anyone else in the school.

I couldn't bear losing a race! Losing a race was unthinkable! You could only lose a race because you didn't run fast enough. I just had to run faster. I even won money by winning races!

My first victory had been in the races at Fawler during the Coronation celebrations. I won half a crown! I had to beat my ginger–headed near–twin in the run off because it had been declared a dead heat!

I wasn't so good at the sack race, the egg and spoon race or the obstacle race but I was okay in the relay race. Even if the other members of the relay team dawdled down the track, I won my 'leg' and that was what mattered.

One day a new boy came to Finstock School and he could run faster than me! I hated him! It was not fair! How could he win when I was running just as fast as I could make my legs run!

Then, quite by chance, and I don't know why, probably because I had forgotten my plimsolls, I ran bare foot and beat him! I could beat him! I could actually run faster than he could! All was right with the world and normality had been restored. Later, when he was about fourteen, he was cycling to Witney when he swerved to avoid a beer delivery lorry coming out of a pub carpark on a bend, straight into an on–coming car. His grave is in Finstock Church graveyard. He was a clever, confident, intelligent, happy–go–lucky kid with everything to look forward too. He deserved something better.

One day Finstock School took part in a county sports day. We had to go to a village with the strange name 'Islip', where there were children from 'Kidlington', 'Eynsham', 'Yarnton' and other faraway places with strange sounding names. We had to wear numbers pinned to our shirts. Some of the children had smart white running shorts and vests! And even spiked running shoes! Running shoes!

In my newly–whited plimsolls I came second! It was because I didn't have running shoes and only had my normal school short trousers and this week's shirt! Had I had white shorts and a white vest and running shoes I would have won by a mile! Anyway, spiked running shoes are useless and just nail your feet to the ground!

It was not until I went to Spendlove Secondary School that I began to take athletics seriously. One supply teacher had been a sprinter and had run for Wales as a student. He taught me to do a racing start, even though we never had starting blocks.

By the age of fourteen I had a 'county standard' in every event, even shotput and discus. I proudly looked at the table on the changing–room notice board as yet another event was ticked off as I achieved another county standard! I had even been timed with a stop–watch and had been started with a starting pistol!

I could not bear to lose!

In one practice relay race I ran last in my team. I took the baton last and flew the 100 yards last leg, passing the leader with about 10 yards to go. I felt my legs driving like pistons beneath me as I past him and hit the tape a second later! I then experience serious oxygen deficit for the first time in my life!

My face maintained a curious rictus of determination, muscles frozen and cramped, unable to relax. I felt dizzy! I couldn't talk! I thought I was dying! I lay on the ground unable to breathe deeply enough and gasping for breath as people crowded around and the sports teacher crouched over me telling me to take really deep breaths! I was! I was breathing as deeply as I could but it wasn't enough! My legs were drawn up and cramped, my calf muscles knotted and painful.

Gradually though, I felt less breathless and started to relax. A curious feeling of softness, of muscles relaxing and the blood coming back into my face overcame me. I was expelling the last of the lactic acid that had built up in my muscles as I had sprinted the last 50 yards or so without taking a breath! I had put so much concentration into running that I had forgotten to breathe! My muscles had burned the stored oxygen in my muscles and then gone into anoxic respiration mode, burning sugar without enough oxygen and making lactic acid instead of carbon dioxide. It was an oxygen deficit my body had to repay as soon as possible before my brain suffered a loss of oxygen and shut down.

"You need to learn to control your breathing!" said the sports teacher, superfluously.

I couldn't bear to lose!

On one occasion I had forgotten my sports kit (actually, my Boy Scout shorts and plimsolls) and had to run in my normal school clothes. I had lost a button on the flies of my grey flannel regulation trousers. My manhood decided this was the ideal time and place to protruded through the gap in my flies and bounce joyously up and down, taking the air and enjoying a few moments freedom as I sprinted for the finish line – with half the school watching.

I managed to push it back in and still won the race.

Did anyone notice? Maybe they were laughing at something else!

"Hey, Bill! Did you know you had yer dick out?" shouted a thoughtful class–mate to general hilarity.

But I had a race to win, and nothing was more important than that! "It's your own fault, you shouldn't have such a big one", said my girlfriend kindly, with an understanding of the male ego far ahead of her time.

In my final sports day, as sports captain for Wychwood House, my House came last. The relay race had been a disaster.

We had had a good team and always won practice races, but on the day our second–best sprinter pulled out and I had to cajole someone else to run. The drop–out had been planned to run first – I was to run last. His replacement refused to run first so I rejigged the team and ran first myself. I had never practiced a baton handover to another runner and I got it completely wrong, held the baton in my right (wrong) hand and tripped my team–mate up! We finished a poor last! Nine whole points missed!

But at least my willy hadn't put in an appearance.

The sports teacher wanted to enter me in county athletics! But,
Spendlove was a Secondary school for children who had failed the 11–
Plus exam and so had been designated as the labourers of the future.
We were to work in the factories, farms and construction industry. We
were at school to learn and not get ideas above ourselves! The head
master vetoed the sports teacher because it would have been a 'waste of
time'. So, my dream, my first real ambition, was waved aside as a
waste of time; not for the likes of these boys!

Anyway, we could never have afforded running shoes!

In The Blink Of An Eye

8. Superstitions and Weather Lore

If Boxing Day on Friday be
A stormy winter we shall see.
Spring will very late appear
And summer cold and wet we fear.

Anon.

In the absence of education, superstition takes over and the countryside ran on superstition. Very much of it having an origin in Christianity of course, but some, like touching wood to prevent bad luck maybe having a pagan origin (although some would say the wood represents the Christian cross).

Superstitions and weather lore were of course not local and there were few superstitions unique to Fawler, never–the–less they played such a fundamental part of our lives that no account of life in Fawler would be complete without some reference to them. Most of the weather lore here comes from our mother who learned it from her shepherd father.

We assumed there were malevolent spirits watching and waiting for us to presume too much, or mention something unpleasant. They would then ensure it happened or would punish us for our presumptuousness.

Mention out loud that there weren't too many cabbage white butterfly caterpillars spoiling your cabbages this year and a plague of cabbage white butterflies was almost guaranteed to descend on your cabbage within a day or two.

Talk openly about cancer or mental illness and someone was bound to succumb to it soon. These malevolent spirits were not too bright, however. Although they could make themselves invisible, suspend the natural laws at will and cause all manner of illnesses and misfortunes, they could be fooled completely if we spoke in hushed tones or used terms like 'Big C' for cancer. We could work out what it meant but they were completely flummoxed by simple codes!

Anything you hoped for was said with 'finger's crossed' and crossed fingers held behind the back protected you against later punishment for telling a fib, but only a little fib or a white lie.

As children, our games were full of incidental superstitions. We could say magic words like 'scrims', 'pax', 'kings' or 'cogs' and we were under a protective spell against being 'got' in a game of tag. It was an eminently 'fair' way to choose someone or pick teams at the start of a game by going through a set ritual. "Eny, meeny, miney, mo…!", "One potato, two potato, three potato, four…!", "Each, peach, pear plumb…!" Something magical was ensuring the outcome was fair or pre–ordained.

On the first of the month, if you remembered to say "white rabbits" before mid–day, you could close your eyes and make a wish and woe betide any child who didn't have an ash twig in their pocket on Ash Wednesday – but only up until mid–day! Failure to comply earned a pinch and a punch. A Pinch and a punch on the first of the month! And no reply! You were now under a protective spell and couldn't be pinched and punched back.

Holly, ivy and mistletoe at Christmas harked back, allegedly, to pre–Christian Druidism and of course the major Christian festivals of Christmas and Easter themselves had pre–Christian origins as mid–winter and spring festivals to do with the return of the sun and to ensure fertility in the planted crops.

A black cat crossing your path meant good luck!

A solitary magpie should be greeted with "Good morning Mr Magpie" and a hat if worn should be doffed. The number of magpies foretold the future: one for sorrow, two for joy; three for a letter, four for something better. Or was it one for sorry, two for joy, three for a girl and four for a boy? It depended where you lived, apparently.

A girl should count the number of plumb or cherry stones after they have eaten their desert and say, "Tinker, taylor, soldier, sailor, rich man, poor man, beggar man, thief", to determine the trade their future husband. They don't seem to have been given much of a choice. But if they could peel a potato or an apple in one go, without breaking the peel, they could throw it over their left shoulder to see the initial of their future husband.

Strangely, the names of my sisters' future husbands were all going to begin with 's', or maybe 'c' or 'g'. Only one married someone whose name began with one of these letters.

Weather lore, in pre–technological times the only way of predicting the weather, was a mixture of experience, plain common sense and superstitions. The best time to plant and harvest were determined partly by phases of the moon and partly by long–term forecasts based on previous weather.

Plant early potatoes on Good Friday! It mattered not whether Good Friday was early or late this year, you still got the earlies in on the right day to ensure a good crop. Main–crop potatoes could wait a few more weeks.

A fog in May means a frost in June – so delay planting tender crops like runner beans and marrows until mid–June. Cast ne'er a clout till May be out! Did this mean the month of May or the blossom of the blackthorn? A clout was a cloak of course. Whatever 'may' meant, you should dress in winter cloths until it was 'out'.

A dripping June keeps everything in tune! Wet early summer meant you could expect a good crop and everything 'coming in' on time.

A frost in May is worth a load of hay!

March comes in like a lion and goes out like a lamb or comes in like a lamb and goes out like a lion. We could expect gales at the start or end of March but never both.

If the ash doth flower before the oak then we should don a winter cloak! If the oak doth flower before the ash then we will have a summer splash. So, not much choice, there; it would either be cold or wet.

One piece of weather lore irritated me no end because it nearly rhymed but not quite:

> The North wind doth blow
> And we shall have snow
> And what will the robin do then, poor thing?
>
> He'll hide in a barn
> And keep himself warm
> And hide his head under his wing, poor thing.

'Barn' and 'warm' don't rhyme! But my mother used to say it when there was a north wind and it looked like snow.

A fairly reliable piece of weather lore, at least in southern England is "Red sky at night; shepherd's delight!" High cloud in the west at sunset to give the 'red sky' presages a fine, dry night. Quite why this should delight shepherds more so than anyone else is anyone's guess. In coastal areas it delights sailors, apparently. A red sky in the morning is naturally a shepherd's warning.

A mackerel sky, not long wet, not long dry! A blue sky dappled with small clouds means changeable weather. Mare's tails (high, wispy stratus clouds) on the other hand means stormy weather is coming.

It goes without saying what the big, black, flat–topped cumulonimbus clouds mean. If you can't see the lightening and hear the thunder, you soon will and it's time to open the downstairs windows and switch off the electrics. Electricity in the house attracts lightening, allegedly. The windows must be open wide so that if a thunder bolt should happen to come down the chimney, it will find the quickest way out. Gran Scarrott always hurried in doors to open her windows at the merest distant rumble of thunder. No point in taking any chances!

The smooth, brown, bolt–shaped fossils of belemnites commonly found in gravel are said to be the remains of old thunder bolts. Everyone knew someone who knew someone who had heard of someone who had a thunderbolt come down their chimney.

Everyone had tales of someone they knew being blown off their feet in a whirlwind or being struck down by hail stones the size of golf balls. I don't recall either of these in Fawler but I was assured there had been, once.

Gulls coming in–land foretells bad weather at sea and probably heading this way. Cows will lay down at the approach of a thunder storm! Cows lay down to chew the cud at about the same time every day anyway, but when they do it before a thunderstorm, well, they're telling us something!

Most houses had a horseshoe nailed to a door post or the lintel to ensure good luck. A horseshoe is believed to represent a new moon and may well be from an earlier religion. Showing your money to a new moon might be from the same source.

Two other things were very likely to be found hanging outside the front door – a pine–cone and a piece of seaweed. Both were believed to foretell rain. Pine cones close up their scales in dry weather and open then in wet weather. This may have some basis in truth as the scales absorb atmospheric moisture.

Seaweed is also believed to go wet when rain is due and to dry out when it isn't. There may also be some basis for this similar to that of pine–cones but a cynic might say seaweed gets wet when it is raining and goes dry when it isn't. It's a great way to tell what the weather is doing now, but not much good at predicting it.

Things happen in threes. The magic number three features often in superstition. It is a prime number, therefore a little bit magical. Rather than being a reference to the Christian triune god it might well be that the triune god is an example of the magic number three.

Of course things happen in threes, depending on where you start counting! They also happen in twos, fours, fives and sixes and any number you choose.

And of course, you never walk under a ladder; a cracked or broken mirror brings seven years bad luck (seven is another magic prime); you never spoke ill of the dead because they might haunt you. Few people doubted that ghosts existed but Fawler was curiously free from ghosts.

Gran Scarrott had a tale about a horse and cart being driven across the frozen village pond and going through the ice, complete with horse and driver, never to be seen again. The pond is a little way away from the main village on the edge of the wood near the disused brick–kiln. It may be the remains of a clay pit but it is reputedly 'bottomless'.

Such an event would normally be guaranteed to produce a ghostly horse and cart, seen on a moonlight night, forever trying to cross the pond, but there was none.

The story was nonsense. There would not have been any reason to drive a horse and cart across the pond which was never known to freeze over anyway. It didn't even freeze in the middle in the severe winter of 1963 when even the River Evenlode froze over enough to skate on. It was actually a mystery why the pond never froze. It had no outlet stream at least on the surface but it never appeared to be stagnant.

The disused brick kiln and buildings in the wood between the hamlet and Fawler Mill would also be expected to produce a clutch of ghosts but never a sign nor even a rumour of one. It was all very disappointing.

One might expect a small hamlet with it Roman connections and with ancient roads now disused and former river bridges now long gone, to have a whole host of ghostly Roman legions, unrequited lovers, lost travellers and itinerant monks roaming the village practically every night at midnight or on a full moon. Maybe we just needed a good tourist board. Perhaps a church or burial ground would have helped.

The best we had was really one belonging to Stonesfield, albeit technically in Fawler.

Outside Stonesfield on the Fawler road is a cross roads near the top of the hill. In the field in the corner of this cross roads is a pile of stones cleared from the field in times gone by. This is "Mary Hill's Grave", reputedly the site of the suicide of Mary Hill, left in the lurch by a lover. Her ghost is said to haunt the cross roads.

Vary many cross roads on the outskirts of towns and villages have 'ghosts' which may be folkloric memories of protective spirits from earlier times. Many people claimed to have seen Mary Hill, including my father.

As you leave Stonesfield, the road goes downhill into a dip before going up to Mary Hill's Grave crossroads. There is a slight double bend in the road as it begins to climb. You can briefly see the road on the far side of the bend as you go down into the dip and then you lose sight of it.

My father swore he saw a figure towards the top of the hill before going into the dip on his way home from work one evening. He was a careful driver who prided himself on his hazards awareness so he prepared to take evasive action to avoid the pedestrian in the road. However, when the road opened up there was no–one there. His workmate who was travelling home with him said "Funny! I could have sworn there was someone in the road!"

Of course, the only possible explanation was that this was Mary Hill.

I walked past Mary Hill's Grave on countless occasions, in daylight and darkness and never saw a thing. Maybe Mary Hill, like so many ghosts, doesn't like sceptics.

The ghost reputedly inhabiting the house we lived in appears to have the same dislike of sceptics as Mary Hill. She supposedly lived in our dining room and couldn't stand the door being shut. You could shut the door and make sure the old lift–catch was in place and maybe half an hour later the latch would lift and the door would creak open. Not fully open, just ajar, but enough to produce a deliciously ghostly slow creak.

I spent many hours with 'Granny' in the dining room doing my school homework at the table and listening to Radio Luxembourg. I would watch the latch and see it gradually slide up and out of the catch. It was loose and twisted at an angle. The catch was worn. The weight of the door, hung slightly out of true, was enough to put pressure on the latch and slight movements in the house were enough to gradually move the latch up and out of the catch. And the door swung open with a creak. A new catch would have been more than enough to keep 'Granny' shut in the dining room.

9. People

We are different people,
From different places,
With different faces,
But deep down one source.
Despite fates deposit,
Like water we float each other's path.

Olujobi Jedidiahz

Fawler of the late 1940s and 1950s was a time when World War was fresh in people's minds.

The sad list of WWII casualties had yet to be added to the war memorials which had sprung up in every village following the dreadful 'war to end wars' that out grandparents had fought and won, only to find their sons fighting on the same battlefields a generation later. Actually, the casualties from Fawler were on the Finstock & Fawler Parish war memorial in Finstock at the Witney Road end of School Road.

We used to read the names as we passed it on the way home from school. Forgive me if I reel them off once more; to ignore them would be an injustice.

From Fawler:
Frederick W. Fowler, Victor C. Hebborn, Philip Paintin, Ralph Taylor.

From Finstock:
Arthur Busby, Ernest Claridge, Frederick C Guy, William Hadland,
Bertram Hunt, Alfred Langford, Frederick Langford, Charles Oliver,
Albert H Pratley, Ernest W. Harris.

Surnames of children we were at school with. Sons and brothers, uncles, lovers and husbands, all disposable and all sacrificed by the hundred thousand for a few yards of territory in a war no–one really understood other than that it was 'for king and country'. They are no longer real people, merely names on a memorial; merely folk memories. None of their wives, mothers, brothers, sisters or children are alive now to remember them.

What would they have become? What did we waste in that primitive barbarism we used to fall back on when diplomacy failed?

The human wrecks of the Flanders trenches and the haunted survivors of The Somme, Passchendaele, Ypres, Verdun, Mons, Vimy Ridge and the many other battlefields of Europe still walked the streets and tried to live as normal lives as they could, daily passing the list of their school friends, brothers, cousins and comrades in arms who never came back.

Mr Swinswood, a kindly, white–haired old man hobbled to the shop and back for an ounce of 'baccer' as best he could; having lost his toes and part of his feet to 'trench–rot'. "Don't you dare laugh at 'im! He got that for his country!" He called me 'Snowball' with a cheery wave because my hair was as white as his.

Mr Johnson. Thin and gaunt, he spoke to no–one and shooed us away when we sang Christmas carols outside his door. "'E's a miserable ol' bugger but 'e must a sin some sights, poor man! 'E were gassed on the Somme! Shell shock!" What did we know of post–traumatic stress disorder?

Some lads who could take no more were shot for cowardice! We never talked about them! What a choice! A firing squad at dawn or the mincing machine of enemy machine guns and artillery! This was their future. This was what their life represented to those who sent them there.

Once a year we stood silent for a minute at 11 o'clock and remembered them!

Les Pilfold, cowman and survivor of a 'Jap' POW camp where several of his starving comrades died from eating boiled tomato leaves. They did not know they were poisonous.

Maurice Crockford, Parachute Regiment. Reputedly the youngest man in the Rhine Crossing, landing in Germany in the Allied advance into the enemy's homeland, in a disposable plywood glider, towed into the air and let go to fare as best it could, flown by a pilot with a few hours training – in how to land. He made wooden model aeroplanes that always faced the wind and with propellers that turned when the wind blew.

Our Dad, Frederick Hounslow, who spent three days on the Dunkirk beach waiting to be rescued. He swam out to a boat three times before finding one with space enough. A transport driver, he had made his way across France with three comrades in the disorderly retreat with order only to 'get to Dunkirk'. Having burned out his lorry when the petrol ran out to stop it getting into enemy hands, they walked the rest of the way or cadged a lift. They survived on what they could take.

Wally Scarrott, master baker and shop–keeper who avoided service on account of being in a reserved occupation. A kindly man who let many a poor family have essentials 'on tick', pay at the end of the week, if you can. We paid for sweets and fizzy pop with cash but everything else, bread, cakes (sometimes as a treat), light bulbs, butter, cheese, sugar, tea… all went 'in the book' and Mum settled up every Friday, after Dad had been paid.

Mrs Creece, farmer's wife, by any standards a snob who spoke in that imperious way 'posh' people do. "Ow yes! Ve'y good." "Yes, DO come in and use the telephone! Shoes owf!" They kept their car in a 'garaaje' while we only had a 'garrije', but no car.

Before the telephone kiosk was installed, the phone at the farm was the only one in the village with which to summon a doctor. We had to "Remember to be polite and say 'please' and 'thankyou' and leave the pennies by the phone!" She would correct our grammar and pronunciation! The men farm–workers were addressed by their surname. But she knew my love of nature and encouraged it and once let me have a paddle in her canoe!

The Oxfordshire countryside was still socially stratified being not greatly different to the days when, a generation earlier, families sent their young girls 'into service' aged fourteen, with instructions to, "Be a good girl and do what the master tells you, mind! I don't want you being sent 'ome without a reference!" Being sent 'ome without a reference' was the worst thing that could happen to a girl because that made her unemployable. She was quite literally at the disposal of the men of the house. Many a young girl came home pregnant, to fend for themselves and their child as best they could. An eighteen year–old caught being used by a son of the house would be instantly dismissed as a 'loose woman', leading him astray.

But at least by the 1950s, with a falling birth–rate and more job opportunities, few girls were sent into service. Many a middle–class housewife found to their cost that 'you just can't get the staff nowadays' and learned to manage without.

Mr Stobo, Farmer. A decent sort who could 'talk the hind–leg off a donkey', who sold me bales of straw for a shilling (for my pigeons) but his wife was an even bigger snob than Mrs Creece. She insisted on being addressed as Ma'am and her two children as 'Miss' and 'Master', even by children of their own age who would have been natural playmates.

They grew up never mixing with the rest of us, though the daughter would ride her pony to within a hundred yards of us and sit watching us. If we called to her, she turned and rode away. On one occasion I realises she was sitting on her pony not twenty yards away watching me sitting under a large elm and enjoying a very private solo activity of the sort adolescent boys often enjoy in private – until she saw I had seen her. I would love to have known her thoughts! Clearly, she thought there was something worth watching.

Mrs Franklin. A widow who gave Mum a jar of goose grease to rub on my chest when, four weeks old, I was at Death's door from pneumonia in the winter of 1947. It saved my life – according to my mother! Mrs Franklin was always the lady who saved my life and her old wrinkled face lit up is a broad, toothless smile when she saw me. She called me 'my Billy'. She believed she saved my life too.

Mrs Pratley, the granddaughter of Lincolnshire pea pickers who were reputedly married by 'jumping the broomstick', who took no nonsense from anyone and could strip her husband's motorbike down in the morning, give it a decoke, fit new piston rings and have it working by teatime.

Mrs Claridge. Always laughing, probably to hide something that was no laughing matter. She and Mrs Pratley, along with Mrs Johnson and Mrs Swinswood, would be out 'spud bashing' as soon as the potato crop was ready. With a hessian sack tied round their waste with 'bag tie' as an apron, with mud–caked clothes and hands they would follow the tractor bent double and picking up the 'spuds' into the apron until it was full, then shoot it into a sack. They would descend on a fallen elm bough; saw in hand, to fill an old pram with firewood for the winter.

Gran Scarrott. Wally's mother who often served in the shop. If there
was no–one in the shop you stood in the yard and called Gran, or went
up to her house to get her. She said "baint" and "bisn't" and "wot be
you a–doing, then?" in normal speech, but then she came from
Stonesfield, about two miles away, where they 'spoke funny' anyway.

Granny Stewart! She probably should have been in care. She would sit
on the village green, sans underwear, legs akimbo, 'taking the air', and
seemingly oblivious of the sniggering children making excuses for

walking past and pretending not to look. She farted loudly too to general merriment!

Granny and Grampy Crockford, who were always arguing but had managed to produce about twelve children. After knocking at their door you would hear a free and frank 'discussion' in the choicest terms about who should answer it. Swearing to them was an art–form! I would have loved to have seen them answer the door to the vicar.

Harry Griffin, whose wife Thora had been taken away screaming in an ambulance. He had a large collection of beautiful Neolithic arrow–heads which he had picked up in a field near Stonesfield – but he would never tell us exactly where! I would have spent hours scouring the field, practically on my hands and knees, just to find a flint arrow–head. Harry was the man you took a litter of kittens or a sick cat too if you wanted them 'taken care of'. He was no vet!

Mr and Mrs Tester who lived opposite us. Mrs Tester was massive. We were told she had 'gland problems'. She always seemed angry and frequently shouted at us from her window. If a ball went over their garden wall it was lost for good. She was more or less isolated in her house as there were several steps down to the front door and garden which she had to climb with great difficulty to get out.

Mr Tester was a small man in every sense of the word. One evening our father had to go out to break up a fight between him and one of the residents on The Green. It started over an argument about who should give way as The Lane was too narrow to allow two cars to pass. Mr Tester had somehow convinced himself that he owned the road outside his house and adjacent to his garden. This amounted to almost half the road. Dad, who was well over six feet tall, was a giant by comparison, had to manhandle him to take an axe off him. To settle the dispute, Dad got in Mr Tester's car and drove it, one wheel on the grass bank, past the other car.

Not from Fawler but very much an honorary Fawlerian when he moved in for a week or two every year, sometime twice in the same year and always a great pleasure to have living there, was Fred Able, the Donkey Man. Fred earned his living travelling around the Midlands with his two donkeys, his dog, assorted mice and rats and an ancient wind–up gramophone and a few vinyl records. He called himself a one man circus. In the early days he gave rides in his cart for a few pence.

He talked with a stammer and repeated himself a lot. Rumour was, and it may have been apocryphal, that he was shell–shocked in the war and had been unable to settle down, opting for a roaming existence, mostly with himself and his animals for company. He spoke with a Norfolk accent.

He was kind to us children when we went along to see him, often finding him cooking on an open fire. He always seemed to be boiling potatoes in a fire–blackened saucepan.

ooOoo

His tent was a large dome–shaped, beige tarpaulin. Soon a fire was lit and a kettle sat on top of it. We used to go along to see him and he did tricks with his dogs, making them sit up and beg, or stand on their hind legs and dance. Even funnier, he used to dress them up in an old coat with a pair of glasses on and a pipe in their mouths. The dogs were so docile. They just sat up and begged and looked so funny. We thought this was so clever.

The best thing was when he walked with his donkeys and a little cart into the village ringing his bell shouting "any rides", We ran up to The Cross and waited our turn to either have a ride in the cart or, if you were brave, a ride on the donkey's back. Lifting us up one at a time and making sure we were safe, he took us past the farm and up to the top of Mill Lane and back. I think he charged six pence ago. This was the only time we had a ride on a donkey. We never went to the sea side or anything like that.

ooOoo

He usually set up camp along Northleigh Lane but later moved to a wide grass verge near the allotments on the Charlbury road. It was here that he built a shelter out of straw bales donated by the farm and endured the long hard winter of 1963. Fred Lake kept an eye on him and no–one begrudged him a few vegetables from the allotments.

Then, one morning when the weather improved, he was gone. He never normally seemed to stay anywhere for more than a week or two. We were flattered that he had chosen Fawler in which to stick out the worst winter in living memory. It made Fred ours, somehow. Such was Fred's popularity that a brief Google search will bring up several newspaper articles from all over the Midlands, and many fond memories and even a few snippets of film of the Fred Able, the Donkey Man.

There were other people and families who it's probably neither wise nor fair to mention in this book. They lived dysfunctional lives behind closed doors having had dysfunctional role–models themselves. Some quietly went insane either through neglect or boredom, or both. Some things were never mentioned or were talked about by adults in hushed tones.

It was by no means an idyllic childhood for some of our friends. Imagine a birthday with no present from your mother who doesn't know what day of the week it is!

Marriage then was mostly for life. Divorce was rare and scandalous and there had to be a 'guilty party'. Women could only escape an abusive relationship with great difficulty and most people thought it was her sacred duty to stick to her marriage vows.

And what happened behind closed doors was private! It was nothing to do with anyone else, not even the police or social services. You did not interfere in other folks' family matters! So abuses of the most grotesque kind went unchecked; by no means in all, or even most families, but certainly in a few. Some will still bear the mental scars.

In The Blink Of An Eye

10. And Then Everything Changed

Come mothers and fathers
Throughout the land,
And don't criticize
What you can't understand.

Bob Dylan

It was in the middle of the summer of 1959 that my parents had taken the plunge and rented a 'telly' from the electrical shop in Chipping Norton. Not many people could afford to buy a television set outright and, as the man in the shop said, what would happen if it went wrong? All that money wasted! A rented set would be replaced at no cost and after three years we could have a new one too for only a small increase in rent!

We bought that television set maybe two or three times over, but at least we had no repair bills!

Before television began to take off in the mid–1950s our evening entertainment was the 'wireless'. This was family Britain where we all listened to the same wireless programs and laughed at the same comedies – the Goons, Ted Ray, Arthur Askey, The Navy Lark, Kenneth Horne.

The great comedy writers of the 1960s cut their teeth writing for the wireless – Bill Oddie, John Cleese, Tim Brook–Taylor and Graham Garden, Dennis Norden and Frank Muir, Bob Monkhouse and Dennis Goodwin, and many, many more. It was on the wireless that the anarchistic British humour of the 1960s was born with such comic geniuses as Spike Milligan, Peter Sellers, Michael Palin and Eric Idle.

We laughed knowingly at the daring Polari *double entendres* of Kenneth William and Hugh Paddick as Julian and Sandy, an obviously camp couple when homosexuality was still a criminal offence. We fell about at the childlike naivety of Ron and Eth, the mischievous antics of The Clitheroe Kid and the soppy northern stupidity of Ken Platt when being a 'soppy northerner' was the equal of the chirpy cocky cockney for comedic value.

To begin with, the only television broadcasts were by the BBC for which you needed an 'H'–shaped aerial mounted on a high–point, usually a chimney. Then 'commercial' television came on line, and with a marketing genius, they needed a different aerial so having 'commercial' became a visible status symbol.

The launch night of ITV was a bit of a flop though. Although they denied it, the BBC planned a spoiler edition of *The Archers*, 'an every–day story of country folk' that I later came to loath as the parody of country life it became. *The Archers* was compulsive family listening, at least in our house. We had to sit quietly when *The Archers* was on.

Instead of tuning in to watch the launch of ITV, we all sat transfixed and horrified as Grace Archer died in that terrible fire in the stables, trying to rescue her beloved horse! They even played a different, solemn signature tune at the end! It was probably the most memorable wireless program ever broadcast in Britain. For years people could remember where they were the night Grace Archer died. Not really that hard because the chances are they were home listening to the wireless!

I knew we were getting a telly delivered but it was not until I strolled up the lane from the village green as it was getting dark and noticed that there was a strange, ghostly, flickering silver-blue light through the crack in the curtains that I really realised we had one. And there was the 'H' on the chimney with the long 'Commercial' aerial too, to tell the world we had a telly with BBC **and** ITV!

Raymond Chandler's, *The Big Sleep* was on and I had to be quiet – and stop walking in front of the telly! Just sit still! For the first time we couldn't just wander about the room at will without being shouted at!

Within a year, maybe much less, we had got into the routine of having dinner at six o'clock and settling down to watch the evening's offering – whatever it was. Later still, dinner would be eaten in front of the telly. We stopped being a family that laid the table for meals and sat round it to eat.

In this Family Britain now everyone watched either BBC or ITV and talked about what they had seen next day at work or school. We all saw the same things and shared in the same experiences just as we had done when the radio was the family entertainment with its choice of three programmes. Those who didn't have a telly were left out.

The social pressures to get a telly built up to become almost irresistible so that by about 1965 almost no–one was without a television and no chimney was free from a TV aerial. A television set was no longer a luxury but an essential. Children stopped playing outside of an evening and so began the move to the full domestication of childhood.

The first televisions had often been bought for the older people by their children, 'to keep them company'. I believe the first one we ever saw was on a visit to relatives in Bromley, Kent, but the first one in the village had been provided for an old couple by their very large family. This was where my best friend lived with his grandparents and where we watched the 1958 World Cup final on a flickering black and white screen.

Static, long–distance cameras filmed black and white blobs as they moved about the football field, amongst them being a 17 year–old Pele. "Please do not adjust your set, there is a break in transmission" could have been the motto for an outside broadcast from as far afield as Sweden. I knew little of football but my best friend, who was later to have trials for Witney Town and Oxford City, was fanatical about the game and kept jumping up and down. Brazil won.

Before long the conversation at school became last–night's television – Quiz shows like *Double Your Money*; American comedies such as *Bilko* or Friday night cowboy shows like *Wagon Train* and *Gun Smoke*. One American comedy starred a strange woman called Lucille Ball who apparently was about fifty years old, but looked like a sixty–five year–old trying to look eighteen. She seemed to be a bit retarded.

Friday evening was cowboy night at 5.30. I had a friend, a boy in foster care, whose carer had a television, so, as a special treat to him as much as to me, I was allowed to go there at exactly 5.30 and watch *The Cisco Kid*, *The Lone Ranger* or whatever was on offer that week. I had to leave as soon as the program ended. How I looked forward to Friday evenings!

Fairly soon the social pressures built up and just about every family had a television, and life changed.

One bonfire night we young teenagers had sloped off up The Lane to The Cross where we were generally chatting and snogging, as we called kissing and petting and generally getting to know one another. I don't remember the program – probably some American cops and robbers series – but suddenly, just as I thought things were progressing nicely with a girl, she suddenly checked her watch and said she had to go because this program was about to start, and ran off down The Lane.

And that was that. I never got that close with her again and it seems to be a metaphor for the changing village life. It all depended on what was on telly! It wasn't now a matter of who was out and about and what we did, but of whether anyone was out and about.

The village died and everyone stayed home and watched television. Maybe I'm being a sentimental old buzzard harking back to some largely illusory good ol' days when small communities were communities in the real sense of the word. A time when everyone knew everyone and the children played outdoors together; more feral than domesticated and more hunter–gatherer than civilised, urbanised. In many ways, more like an extended family.

The advent of television, even more so that the advent of the radio, the motor car and computers probably did more to change and largely destroy the ages–old way of life of the small English rural communities, than a couple of centuries of industrialisation and mechanisation ever did.

There were two other events which were to have a major influence not just on me and my generation but on British society and social attitudes: the Profumo Affair and the Lady Chatterly, obscene publications trial.

The Profumo affair concerned the then Minister for War, John Profumo, a senior member of Harold MacMillan's Tory government, and his relationship with 'society prostitutes', Christine Keeler and Mandy Rice–Davies. Suddenly the news was full of words like 'call–girl' and accounts of sexual behaviour and casual promiscuity amongst the upper classes that had been strictly taboo subjects in a more deferential age. At school we excitedly discussed what a call–girls was and did and how the private behaviour of the 'nobs' was so different to their public pretences.

It was the beginning of the end of the deferential society where seigneurial, born to rule Tories, produced on the playing fields of Eton and Rugby, decided what was best for the masses and we gratefully kowtowed and thanked them for their kindness. Very quickly, the upper classes became objects of fun and derision with stage shows such as *Beyond the Fringe* mercilessly mocking the upper classes, followed by the age of satire with television programs like *That Was The Week That Was*, which became compulsive Saturday evening viewing, and in which the political establishment was mocked and satirised to the delight of us all.

The Lady Chatterley trial, where Penguin Books was put on trial under the Obscene Publications Act for publishing the previously banned D. H. Lawrence novel, *Lady Chatterley's Lover. Lady C*, as it quickly became known, described in explicit detail the sexual activity between an aristocratic married lady and her game–keeper.

The shocking thing, from the point of view of the ruling establishment was not so much the explicit language used but the fact that it described a sexual relationship between an aristocrat and a servant. Famously, the prosecution barrister, in his opening statement to the jury had asked them to consider if this was a book they would like their wife or servant to read! This was met with incredulous laughter in court even from the jury, summarising as it did all that seemed wrong with a hierarchical society. A society in which women and servants could and should have their decisions made for them by upper–class men who naturally knew best.

Penguin Books won the case after we, as adolescents, had been treated to yet another dose of sexually explicit news items and very soon passages describing activities that had never before occurred to us, but which we couldn't wait to try for ourselves, were being bandied about. Previous taboos had been broken and the unthinkable was becoming thinkable.

Sexual activity which had always been going on in strict privacy was now openly talked about. Sex was ceasing to be something done with guilt and becoming something taken for granted as a normal part of male/female relationship. It only needed the contraceptive pill to liberate women from the fear of pregnancy and sex became the healthy, recreational activity it should always have been had it not been for the sanctimonious interference of religious superstition.

So we went into the 1960s with the Beatles and Rolling Stones, The Kinks and The Who, Bob Dylan and Joan Baez singing songs of protest and sexual liberation, political revolution and a rejection of the established order.

All we were saying was "Give peace a chance!" Soon no home or teenager's bedroom was complete without a record player and the wealthy ones could afford a stereo record player even though the LPs cost more. Very soon our collection of vinyl LPs came to define us as people maybe even more so than our collection of books.

And a way of life having more in common with 1860 than with 1960 was gone in the blink of an eye.

So that was Fawler.

If you want to see it, leave Stonesfield on the Charlbury road and find Fawler at the bottom of a long down–hill stretch with lovely views across the Evenlode valley, now sadly missing the ancient elms that lined the road and embraced the hamlet, keeping it safe and cosy since times immemorial.

It has a name sign now so you can't miss it. It starts at the right–hand bend where the road from Northleigh joins, and finishes half a mile later where the road to Finstock and Witney forks off to the left.

Drive slowly for there are scruffy ghosts of scruffy children still playing on The Cross and down The Lane to The Green or walking with a bag of corn for the chickens up to the 'lopment' on the Charlbury road.

At least I can still see them.

About the Author

I was born and brought up in the small North Oxfordshire hamlet of Fawler during the post-war baby boom and have had a love of nature since before I can remember. I was one of five children of the daughter of a Cotswold shepherd of some renown, and a car factory worker and former soldier who was rescued from Dunkirk and spent the last three years of World War II in India where he learned to speak Hindi.

By any standards we were poor and grew most of the food we ate in our garden and on an allotment on the edge of the village. In some respects we were close to hunter-gatherers and along with other villagers, never passed over a chance to gather firewood from the woods and fields when a large elm tree fell or shed a branch, to collect watercress from the River Evenlode and to gather mushrooms and wild fruit from the fields and hedgerows in autumn.

I don't remember learning to read – I was probably about five or six years old – but I read anything I could get my hands on, especially anything to do with nature. I realised I was an atheist when I was nine years old when it suddenly dawned on me that not all religions could be right, but they could all be wrong. Since there was no more reason to suppose only ours was right while all the others, ancient and modern, were wrong, the most sensible view was that they were all wrong. I have been an atheist ever since.

On leaving school with a few 'O' levels, I worked as a laboratory technician for Oxford University on a Medical Research Council grant, working my way up to Senior Research Technician and gaining an ONC in Science, HNC in Applied Biology and state registration as a Medical Laboratory Technician. I co-authored a paper on reproductive physiology in guinea pigs in the process.

After eleven years I was made redundant when the government cut back on research spending and our small unit was disbanded. Disillusioned and needing a job to support a new family, I decided on a change of career and joined the Ambulance Service. With the advantage my medical and biological knowledge gave me I became one of the first UK Paramedics and an instructor, eventually working my way through the ranks to become a Control Room Manager.

I gained a Diploma In Management Studies at Oxford Brookes University, taught myself computer programming and became the Trust's Information Manager and Freedom of Information and Data Protection Officer. I formally retired two years early but was asked to return part-time as a performance information analyst and deployment planning consultant. I finally retired completely about 18 months ago and now spend my time writing my *Rosa Rubicondior* blog on science and religion and occasionally on politics, and researching my family tree.

My blog can be found at https://rosarubicondior.blogspot.co.uk.

I have been a socialist and trades unionist since my teens and have been a member of the Labour Party for about thirty years. I am a keen supporter of the European Union as a better way of doing business between neighbouring countries. Briefly, during the early 1970s, I was a member of the Communist Party of Great Britain but left after a couple of years when I realised it was as dogmatic and cult-like as a fundamentalist religion; quite incapable of holding rational debates about policy or changing to meet the changing needs of a post-industrial economy.

Within twenty years, Communist regimes in Eastern Europe were collapsing under their own inertia and irrelevance and the people of Eastern Europe were taking their countries back. Like religions, Communism was never anything more than a promise of jam tomorrow.

So that's me: a materialist rationalist who never consciously decided to be led by evidence but who has always assumed that it is the only honest thing to do. I think the Universe is wonderful enough without magic and mystery.

Under the name *Rosa Rubicondior*, I have published several books of compilations of my blog posts and a wholly original book, *Ten Reasons To Lose Faith: And Why You Are Better Off Without It.* I have since added two more titles dealing with the anti-science cult of Creationism *The Unintelligent Designer: Refuting the Intelligent Design Hoax,* and *The Malevolent Designer: Why Nature's God is not Good.* Also available is *A History of Ireland: How Religion Poisoned Everything.*

These books are available from Amazon in paperback, hardcover and ebook for Kindle versions.

Other Books by the Author
(Writing as Rosa Rubicondior)

The Light of Reason Series:

The Light of Reason: And Other Atheist Writings.

Irreverent essays, thought-provoking articles and humorous items on atheism, religion, science, evolution, creationism and related issues.

(Paperback) ISBN-10: 1516906888, ISBN-13: 978-1516906888	£9.95 (US $14.95)
(Kindle) ASIN: B014N0IPVI	£3.95 (US $5.99)

The Light of Reason: Volume II – Atheism, Science and Evolution.

Thought-provoking essays on the conflict between fundamentalist religion and science, and exposing the anti-science, extremist political agenda of the modern creationist industry.

(Paperback) ISBN-10: 1517105188, ISBN-13: 978-1517105181	£9.95 (US $14.95)
(Kindle) ASIN: B014N0IR16	£3.99 (US $5.99)

The Light of Reason: Volume III – Apologetics, Fallacies, and Other Frauds.

Thought-provoking essays and articles on religion and atheism, dealing with religious apologetics, fallacies, miracles and other frauds

(Paperback) ISBN-10: 151710761X, ISBN-13: 978-1517107611	£6.95 (US $9.95)
(Kindle) ASIN: B014N0IRE8	£2.99 (US $3.99)

The Light of Reason: Volume IV - The Silly Bible.

Exposing the absurdities, contradictions and historical inaccuracies in the Bible and advancing the case for atheism and against religion. This volume, the fourth in the Light of Reason series, deals with contradictions and absurdities in the Bible.

(Paperback) ISBN-10: 1517108209, ISBN-13: 978-1517108205	£8.95 (US $13.95)
(Kindle) ASIN: B014N0IR8E	£3.99 (US $4.99)

The Light of Reason: And Other Atheist Writing. (all 4 volumes in one book)

Based on the Rosa Rubicondior science and Atheism blog, this is a collection of Atheist and science articles, some short, others lengthier, exploring the interface between religion and science and which have been published over some four years.

(Kindle only) ASIN: B013DYOK32	£6.34 (US $9.95)

Other books on science, Atheism and theology

An Unprejudiced Mind: Atheism, Science & Reason.

Essays on science and theology from a scientific atheist perspective, exploring particularly evolution versus creationism.

(Paperback) ISBN-10: 1522925805, ISBN-13: 978-1522925804	£9.95 (US $14.95)
(Kindle) ASIN: B019UGXPM4	£3.99 (US $5.95)

The Unintelligent Designer: Refuting the Intelligent Design Hoax

Showing with examples from biology why there is no evidence of design, intelligent or otherwise and illustrating how any designer who would design so ineptly could not be described as benevolent.

(Paperback) ISBN–10: 1723144215, ISBN–13: 978-1723144219   £8.45 (US $10.75)
(Kindle). ASIN: B07G121BMK   £4.55 (US $5.95)

Ten Reasons To Lose Faith: And Why You Are Better Off Without It.

Why faith is not only a fallacy and useless as a route to the truth but is actually harmful to society and to the individual. It systematically dismantles the standard religious apologetics and shows them to be bogus and deliberately constructed to mislead.

(Paperback). ISBN-13:978-1530431953, ISBN-10: 1530431956   £10.75 (US $14.75)
(Kindle) ASIN: B01DGVO3JS   £6.95 (US $8.95)

What Makes You So Special? : From the Big Bang to You.

How did you come to be here, now? This book takes you from the Big Bang to the evolution of modern humans and the history of human cultures

(Paperback), ISBN-13: 978-1546788294, ISBN-10: 1546788298   £8.95 (US $11.50)
(Kindle).ASIN: B071FTKXLZ $6.20 (US $8.25)

A History of Ireland: How Religion Poisoned.

From the earliest times religion has shaped Ireland and divided Irishman against Irishman (and woman) culminating in the 'troubles' between Protestants Loyalists and Catholics Nationalists in Northern Ireland in the 1960's and 70's. and still festers in the background This brief history describes how religion was the background to the 'Troubles'

(Paperback), ISBN-13: 978-1724988492; SBN-10 : 1724988492   £8.90 (US $11.00)
(Hardcover), ISBN-13 : 979-8507235032   £14.60 (US $18.00)
(Kindle), ASIN : B07HHHRB34   £5.30 (UD $6.50)

The Internet Creationists' Handbook : A Joke for the Rest of Us.

A humorous look at creationist apologetics on the Internet, showing the fallacies and dishonest tactics creationists are using to try to recruit scientifically illiterate people into their political cult.

(Paperback),ISBN-13: 978-1721605149, ISBN-10: 1721605149£5.25   (US $7.50)
(Kindle) ASIN: B07DZF75KD   £3.75 (US $5.00)

The Christian Apologists' Handbook: A Joke for the Rest of Us.

A humorous look at Christian apologetics on the Internet, showing the fallacies and dishonest tactics Christian fundamentalists are using to try to recruit scientifically and theologically illiterate people to their cults, often with political motives.

(Paperback) ISBN-13: 978-1721724727, ISBN–10: 1721724729   £5.25 (US $7.50)
(Kindle) ASIN: B07DYDVMW4   £3.75 (US $5.00)

Books by Rosa Rubicondior

The Muslim Apologists' Handbook: A Joke for the Rest of Us.

A humorous look at Muslim apologetics on the Internet, showing the fallacies and dishonest tactics Muslim fundamentalists are using to try to recruit scientifically and theologically illiterate people to their cuts, often with political motives.

(Paperback) ISBN-13: 978-1721756896, ISBN-10: 1721756892   £5.25 (US $7.50)

(Kindle) ASIN: B07DZF75KD $3.75 (US $5.00)

The author's blog; mostly about science, religion, Atheism and (occasionally) politics: https://rosarubicondior.blogspot.co.uk

Printed in Great Britain
by Amazon